# A FAITH FOR THE YEAR 2000

J ROY H PATERSON

# A FAITH FOR THE YEAR 2000

## A GUIDE TO MEMBERSHIP OF THE CHURCH

THE SAINT ANDREW PRESS

EDINBURGH

First published in 1990 by
THE SAINT ANDREW PRESS
121 George Street, Edinburgh, EH2 4YN

ISBN 0 7152 0639 7

*The Publisher would like to thank
The Westminster/John Knox Press, Louisville, Kentucky
for the use of the hymn by Carol Rose Inkeler (p 25).*

**British Library Cataloguing in Publication Data**
Paterson, J. Roy H.
A faith for the year 2000: a guide to membership of the
church.
1. Christian church
I. Title
260

ISBN 0–7152–0639–7

This book is set in 10/11pt Palatino and 9/10pt Helvetica

Typeset by J&L Composition Ltd, Filey, North Yorkshire
Printed by Bell and Bain Ltd., Glasgow

# Sections on . . .

*To my wife Moyra and our three sons, Stephen, Roger and Brian who have in part been the source of inspiration behind this book.*

# Introduction

This completely new revision of *A Faith for the 1980s* has been written with a view to meeting the needs of the membership of the Church in the twenty-first century. It has taken into account the usefulness of the earlier editions, often presenting this in a fresh and original way, but it has also introduced much new material.

Though written by a Church of Scotland minister, it is not tied to a particular tradition but will be of value to ministers, officebearers and members of many different Churches. For those who wish to use them, there are two different sets of church membership vows on the last page.

The text and layout of this book are simple and straightforward, making it attractive to the general reader, but also valuable to those who are looking for a book they can use in an enquirers' group or at a membership course for instruction and discussion purposes.

# *The wise owl says...*

If you want to know what it means to be a Christian...or a member of the Christian Church

this book will help you to find an answer. It may also make you ask other questions about yourself and what you believe.

In addition to this book, you will need a Bible. Use a good modern translation (see page 47 for list of Bibles with abbreviations). The references in this book are to the GOOD NEWS BIBLE (GNB).

## SOME QUESTIONS TO ASK YOURSELF

Do I believe in God...and if so, what do I mean by it?

If you are not sure about this, ask yourself whether you may be

an **ATHEIST** = someone who believes that there is no God, or
an **AGNOSTIC** = someone who doesn't know if there is a God or not.

Many people come to a belief in God through first being agnostics. They are not denying the possibility, but they want to have an open mind towards it. This book will help you to make up your mind.

# A matter of Belief

## BELIEVING...

We need a belief (or a faith) because we live in two different worlds—
the world of the senses and the world of the unseen. We can see the
world of the senses with our eyes. The unseen world we can only
know by faith. 'To have faith...is to be certain of the things we
cannot see' (Hebrews 11:1). God belongs to the world of the unseen.
'No-one has ever seen God' (1 John 4:12). To know God, we must
have faith.

## IN GOD...

Believing in God is not just believing that there is a God but trusting
him with our lives. I believe in my friend. A friend is someone on
whom I can rely. If at any time I need help, I believe that I will be able
to go to my friend and get help. I cannot prove this, however, until
some need arises and I actually go looking for help.

In the same way I may believe in God, but until I need to go to him for
help or guidance, there is no way of testing my faith. The proof that
we believe in God is that we are able to trust him.

> Our ancestors put their trust in you;
> they trusted you, and you saved them.
>
> (Psalm 22:4).

## WHO HAS MADE HIMSELF KNOWN IN JESUS CHRIST

The Christian faith is not built on a myth or on a fantasy. It is firmly
based on a fact of history—that a man called Jesus of Nazareth lived
in that town some 2000 years ago. Christians believe that God made
himself known in a very special way in this man. He was God
incarnate (= in a body of flesh). John, in his Gospel, describes it thus:
'The Word became a human being' (John 1:14). Or as it is described
in 1 John 1:1, 'We write to you about the Word of life...we have
heard it, we have seen it with our eyes...and our hands have
touched it'. Jesus was God in human form.

3

# Getting to know God

'What are you drawing?' asked a mother of her little girl who was crayoning a picture. 'I'm drawing God,' she replied. 'But no-one knows what God looks like,' said her mother. 'No,' said the child 'but they will when I have finished!'

What is your picture of God? Christians claim to have a unique knowledge of God because of Jesus. Long before Jesus was born, however, God had made himself known through people like the prophet Isaiah.

## THERE IS ONLY ONE GOD

Isaiah taught that there is only one God. Other nations at the time believed in many gods. The God of Israel, said Isaiah, has no rivals. 'I am the Lord; there is no other god' (Isaiah 45:5).

The name 'Lord' (translation of 'Jehovah') means that God has a distinct personality and character. What he does not have is a physical body. 'God is Spirit,' says Jesus (John 4:24). We, however, can have a personal relationship with God because we are also spiritual.

## ...WHO IS SOMETIMES DESCRIBED AS THE TRINITY

The Trinity means that God has made himself known in three different ways—as Father, Son and Holy Spirit.

Long ago an actor would portray different characters on the stage by placing different masks (= in Latin, *personae*) over his face. So God has Three *Personae* or Persons. As **FATHER**, he shows himself to be everywhere and at all times. As the **SON**, he showed himself as Jesus of Nazareth 2000 years ago—there and then. As the **HOLY SPIRIT**, he shows himself to be where we are at the present time—here and now.

# God—the Father

'Father' was Jesus' distinctive name for God but it was also a name by which he was known before Jesus' day.

> As kind as a father is to his children,
> So kind is the Lord to those who honour him.
>
> (Psalm 103:13)

To describe God as Father makes him—not a distant and unknowable God—but a God who can be known and who is 'near to those who call to him' (Psalm 145:18).

The word Jesus used for 'Father' was 'Abba' (Mark 14:36, RSV), the equivalent of 'Dad'. Our relationship with God should be as intimate as that of someone who calls his or her father 'Dad'. St Augustine described the fatherhood of God in this way—'God loves each one of us as though there was only one of us to love'.

The father in the story of the Prodigal Son (Luke 15:11–33) is Jesus' description of God. The father loves his two sons equally but he is especially glad to welcome back the son who has gone off on his own.

## The Son was Sick of Home—then became Home-Sick
The younger son thought he would be happier if he left home and lived his own life. His father gave him money but he soon used it up on 'wine, women and song'. When he was destitute, he wanted nothing more than to return home—but he did not know whether his father would take him back. In the same way, people who live independently of God become restless and unhappy but are not sure if God will welcome them back.

## The Father could not Forget—but was ready to Forgive
The father never forgot his son even though he had cut himself off from him and gone to live in another country. One day he saw him returning home and ran out to meet him. Before his son could say he was sorry, he had thrown his arms round him in welcome. In the same way God is waiting to welcome back those who have been living away from him. He is more ready to forgive us than we are to admit that we have been away.

5

# God—the Father

God is not only Father—he is also Creator. According to the Bible, the world and everything in it was created by God. 'God, the Father who is the Creator of all things' (1 Corinthians 8:6). The Apostles' Creed begins, 'I believe in God the Father Almighty, Maker of heaven and earth'.

The first man to travel in space, the Russian astronaut, Yuri Gagarin, said that in his travels through space he had seen no sign of God. This confirmed his belief that the world was not created by God. On the other hand, one of the first American astronauts to circle the moon read at that point the first four words of Genesis—IN THE BEGINNING, GOD. It is all a matter of belief.

The biblical account of creation is told in Genesis 1:1–31 and 2:1–4. This tells how the world was created in six days. The writers of this story were not scientists. They were not trying to explain *how* the world was made—but *why* it was made. God, they said, made the world and placed us in it so that along with him we might enjoy and appreciate what he had created. After completing creation, 'God looked at everything he had made, and he was very pleased' (Genesis 1:31).

The highest form of life that God created is ourselves. Genesis 1:27 tells us that God created human beings—he created them male and female—making them to be like himself (= in his image, NIV). This was so that we might have fellowship with him and with one another. It is all the more remarkable that a God who could create such a world is also mindful of each one of us. We are reminded of this in Psalm 8, verses 3 and 4.

> When I look at the sky, which you have made,
>> at the moon and the stars, which you set in their places,
> what is man, that you think of him,
>> mere man, that you care for him?

# God—the Father

God not only creates—he also provides for his children. At every moment of every day God as Father Creator is caring for his world and everything in it.

## GOD IN HUMAN HISTORY

A story worth reading is that of Joseph and his brothers in Genesis, chapters 37 and 41 to 46. It is a simple narrative. Joseph was Jacob's favourite son and it made his brothers jealous. They sold him to some traders travelling to Egypt. While there Joseph interpreted a dream of the Pharaoh (= the King). There was going to be a world famine and he must put corn into store. Joseph was put in charge of food supplies. The famine came but the Egyptians were prepared. Then Joseph's brothers came to Egypt looking for corn and they met Joseph—but didn't recognise him. Eventually he told them who he was and invited them to bring his father Jacob to Egypt. There they were all looked after. Later he said, 'You plotted evil against me, but God turned it into good' (Genesis 50:20).

## GOD IN HUMAN LIVES

God gives clear guidance, particularly in Jesus, as to how people ought to live their lives. If they decide to go their own way, however, he does not stop them. He gives us all free wills. As a result some people cause harm to themselves, for example those who drink to excess or take drugs. For some forms of suffering, like the sudden tragedy, the fatal accident, the wasting disease, there is often no human reason or explanation.

Christians believe that 'God works for good with those who love him, those whom he has called according to his purpose' (Romans 8:28). When bad things happen to us, either through some fault of our own or for no good reason, we must trust God who knows and understands the situation. He can bring good out of evil and triumph out of tragedy.

# God—the Son

The events of the Christian Year help us to know the story of Jesus.

**ADVENT**  Advent means 'coming'. An angel who spoke to Mary referred to his coming in this way—'You will ... give birth to a son, and you will name him Jesus' (Luke 1:31). We sometimes also talk about the Second Advent. This refers to the belief that one day Jesus will come again.

**CHRISTMAS DAY**  This marks the birthday of Jesus in Bethlehem. Mary and Joseph had gone there from their home in Nazareth to be registered (Luke 22:4–6). After his birth they went with him to Egypt because they had heard that King Herod wanted to kill Jesus (Matthew 2:13). On Herod's death they returned to Nazareth where Jesus grew up and went to school. At the age of twelve he was taken to Jerusalem for the *bar-mitzva* (= 'son of the law') ceremony (Luke 2:41–52). From then until about the age of thirty, he followed his father's trade as a carpenter in Nazareth.

**LENT**  Lent means 'lengthening' and refers to the month of March when the days lengthen. It marks the forty days that Jesus spent in the wilderness after his baptism in the River Jordan (Mark 1:9–13). For three years after this he went about preaching, teaching and healing—at first in Capernaum and Bethsaida on the Sea of Galilee and later around the Jordan and in Jerusalem.

**PASSION SUNDAY**  'Passion' is another word for 'suffering'. Jesus suffered because from the very beginning there were those who wanted him put to death. The last week of his life is called Holy Week and begins with Palm Sunday when

**PALM SUNDAY**  he rode into Jerusalem on a donkey and the people waved palm branches. On the Thursday he had a last supper with his disciples. Later one of them—Judas—

**GOOD FRIDAY**  betrayed him in the Garden of Gethsemane. He was arrested, put on trial, condemned to death and on Friday he was crucified.

**EASTER DAY**  On the Sunday Jesus was seen alive again by some of his disciples. The tomb where his body had been laid was empty. For forty days thereafter he appeared at various times and in different places to those who had

**ASCENSION**  known him before. After that 'he was taken up to heaven' (Acts 1:9). This is known as the Ascension.

# God—the Son

It is the Christian belief that Jesus was both human and divine. 'God was in Christ' (2 Corinthians 5:19, AV).

## Believing that Jesus was Human

Jesus' neighbours and friends thought of him as one of themselves. In Nazareth he was known as Jesus, son of Joseph the carpenter. He is later referred to as 'the carpenter, the son of Mary, and the brother of James, Joseph, Judas and Simon' (Mark 6:3). He lived a normal human life. The name he chose for himself was 'Son of Man'.

## Believing that Jesus is Divine

Though Mary was his natural mother, it is suggested in Matthew 1:18 that Joseph may not have been his natural father. 'His mother Mary was engaged to Joseph but before they were married, she found out that she was going to have a baby by the Holy Spirit'. This may have been Matthew's way of saying that Jesus was also the 'Son of God'.

Certainly his disciples who lived and worked with him realised that he was not like one of them. A later writer commented that 'he was tempted in every way that we are, but did not sin' (Hebrews 4:15). One day Simon Peter declared openly that he was 'the Christ, the Son of the living God' (Matthew 16:16).

What was it that made him and the others believe that Jesus was divine?

(a) *What he taught*
'The crowd was amazed at the way he taught. He wasn't like the teachers of the Law; instead he taught with authority' (Matthew 7:29).

(b) *What he claimed*
He said things that only God would have had a right to say, for example 'I am the way, the truth and the life; no one goes to the Father except by me' (John 14:6).

(c) *What he did*
He performed miracles (= wonderful things). He healed people who were ill. He even forgave those who had sinned and everyone knew that 'God is the only one who can forgive sins' (Mark 2:7).

9

# God—the Son

In what ways can we speak about Jesus as the Son of God?

## A Son has a Likeness to his Father

An onlooker may see a baby boy in his pram and say, 'He's very like his father!' What the person sees is a physical resemblance. When Jesus said, 'Whoever has seen me has seen the Father' (John 14:9), he was referring to a character likeness. To a Jew, 'son of' meant 'having the same nature as'.

---

### CAMERA OBSCURA

On Castle Hill below Edinburgh Castle there is the Outlook Tower with its Camera Obscura. By means of an angled lens on the roof, visitors are able to see on a table beside them a bird's-eye view of surrounding Edinburgh. In the same way, God 'out there' can be seen through Jesus who is 'beside us'. He 'reflects the brightness of God's glory and is the exact likeness of God's own being' (Hebrews 1:3).

---

## A Son has Access to his Father

If you want to meet someone whom you don't know, it may be possible for you to do this if you know some close relative who will introduce the person to you. Jesus is the one through whom we can meet with God because he is his Son. 'It is through Christ that all of us . . . are able to come . . . into the presence of the Father' (Ephesians 2:18).

# God—the Son

'Jesus Christ is the same yesterday, today and for ever.'
(Hebrews 13:8)

## JESUS CHRIST—In the Beginning

Before history ever began, he was the agent through whom God made the universe. 'Through him God created everything in heaven and on earth, the seen and the unseen' (Colossians 1:16).

## JESUS CHRIST—There and Then

Jesus lived in a particular country [modern Israel] and at a particular time in history [approximately 2000 years ago]. Everything that happened before is referred to as BC (Before Christ) and everything that happened afterwards as AD (*anno Domini* = In the Year of our Lord). The story of Jesus' birth, life, death and resurrection is told on page 8.

## JESUS CHRIST—Here and Now

The biblical picture of Jesus now is of one who has risen, ascended and 'sits on his throne at the right hand side of God' (Colossians 3:1). The right hand of God is the place of honour. He sits because he has completed the work God gave him to do in this world. Now because he knows what our human life is like, he acts like an advocate and pleads our cause before God (Romans 8:34).

## JESUS CHRIST—At the End

As the world began, so it must end. No-one knows when that will be. During his lifetime Jesus said, 'You do not know the day or the hour' (Matthew 25:13). On *that* day, we are told, the Son of Man will come and 'judge the living and the dead' (2 Timothy 4:1) according to how they have lived their lives—whether or not they have cared for the hungry, the homeless and the destitute. Read the story in Matthew 25:32–46.

# God—the Holy Spirit

SPIRIT in the original Hebrew and Greek languages meant BREATH or WIND.

In the New Testament the SPIRIT is often referred to as the HOLY SPIRIT.

## GOD'S SPIRIT AS BREATH

Job said, 'God's Spirit made me and gave me life' (Job 33:4).

After his resurrection, Jesus appeared to his disciples on the Sunday evening, breathed on them and said, 'Receive the Holy Spirit' (John 20:22).

There is a hymn about the Holy Spirit that begins thus:

> Breathe on me, breath of God,
> Fill me with life anew.

## GOD'S SPIRIT AS THE WIND

In the story of creation in Genesis 1:2, it says that the Spirit of God [or a wind from God] 'was moving over the water'.

There is mystery about the wind because it is its own master. Jesus said to Nicodemus one night, 'The wind blows wherever it wishes; you hear the sound it makes, but you do not know where it comes from or where it is going. It is like that with everyone who is born of the Spirit' (John 3:8). God's Spirit blows in upon peoples' lives in different ways—stirring their consciences, inspiring their thoughts and giving them direction for their lives.

On the Festival of Pentecost (= Fiftieth Day after Passover), the Holy Spirit came 'like a strong wind blowing' (Acts 2:2) among those who had gathered in Jerusalem. Many became aware of a new power in their lives. They found they were able to speak in other languages (= possibly the same as the phenomenon of speaking with tongues), and to preach and to heal in the name of Jesus Christ.

12

# God—the Holy Spirit

The dove has always been regarded by Christians as a symbol of the Spirit. After his baptism in the Jordan, Jesus said that 'he saw heaven opening and the Spirit coming down on him like a dove' (Mark 1:10). He interpreted this as a sign that God was now ready for him to begin his work of proclaiming God's Kingdom.

The Holy Spirit particularly refers to that Person of the Trinity who Jesus said would act for him after he had gone from the earth. At the last supper he told his disciples about the Holy Spirit. His words are recorded for us in John, chapters 14 to 17.

## THE HOLY SPIRIT IS AN AMBASSADOR
An ambassador is one who officially represents his or her country in someone else's country. As ambassadors must always speak for their own country, so the Holy Spirit must always speak for Jesus. 'He will not speak on his own authority,' said Jesus 'but he will speak of what he hears . . . he will give me glory, because he will take what I say and tell it to you' (John 16:13,14).

## THE HOLY SPIRIT AS TEACHER
A teacher puts across a lesson in a way that the pupil will understand. Similarly the Holy Spirit makes clear to us the words of Jesus. He 'will teach you everything and make you remember all that I have told you,' said Jesus (John 14:26).

## THE HOLY SPIRIT AS HELPER
A helper is someone who gives assistance when it is needed. The word for this in John's Gospel is also used of a tug that comes alongside a big ship to help her navigate a narrow channel. In the AV translation, the word 'Comforter' is used. Originally this meant, not someone who consoles us, but someone who helps us to be strong. The NEB translation uses the word 'Advocate' meaning someone who helps us by pleading for us. 'I will ask the the Father,' says Jesus, 'and he will give you another to be your Advocate, who will be with you for ever' (John 14:16, NEB).

13

# Looking in the Mirror

It is now time for you to ask some questions of yourself.

'O wad some Pow'r the giftie gie us to see oursels as others see us!' wrote Robert Burns.

If you look in a mirror you will have some idea of what people see when they look at you! In James 1:23ff we are told about 'a man who looks in a mirror and sees himself and then at once forgets what he looks like'. James says this is like someone who hears God speaking to him, knows very well what he is saying to him but doesn't really want to hear.

So often when we look at ourselves, we see the people we like to think we are—and not the people we actually are. Oliver Cromwell once asked the Dutch artist, Peter Lely to paint his portrait. 'Do not flatter me at all,' he said, 'but leave in all these roughnesses, pimples, warts, and everything as you see me—otherwise I will never pay a farthing [a quarter of an old penny] for it'.

## MIRROR QUESTIONS—to help you find out about yourself!

What kind of impression do you give of yourself to other people, for example your parents, your children, your teacher, your boss, those who work with you or for you, those with whom you spend your leisure time?

What TV programmes do you watch? What kind of music do you enjoy? What type of work interests you? What sports or hobbies do you have? Now what do the answers tell you about yourself?

What kind of things make you happy and what kind of things upset you—at home, at school or college or university, at work or among your friends? Why do they have this effect on you?

14

# Reflections in God's Mirror

Let us think of Jesus Christ as the image of God and of ourselves as reflected in that mirror. Here are three stories about people who began to see themselves as they really were when they looked into this particular mirror. Do you see your own reflection in any of these pictures?

## A YOUNG MAN WHO WAS UNSETTLED (Mark 10:17–22)

He had everything that money could buy. He was well off but he wasn't happy. One day he said to Jesus, 'Good Teacher, what must I do to receive eternal life [= peace of mind]?' Jesus told him to keep the commandments. He had always done this. Then sell all your possessions, Jesus told him, and give the money to help the poor. His possessions, however, were too important to him and he went away still unhappy. Does owning things sometimes make us discontented?

## A WOMAN WHO HAD MESSED THINGS UP (John 4:1–30)

This woman had got a bad name for herself. The other women in the village wouldn't let her draw water from their well. She walked to a well two miles out of the village and there she met Jesus. After a short conversation, she discovered that he knew all about her past, that she had been married five times and that she was now living with a man who was not her husband. Despite this he didn't condemn her and she went back to the village feeling for the first time forgiven and free. Does knowing that someone cares for us, despite the kind of lives we have lived, help us to change and make a fresh start?

## A MAN WHO HAD NO FRIENDS (Luke 19:1–10)

Zacchaeus was a tax-collector employed by the Roman Government. He was hated, mainly because he cheated people of their money. There was nothing he wanted more than friends and so he was overjoyed when Jesus saw him up the tree and asked to come into his house. Is our loneliness sometimes our own fault and does this story show how it can be overcome?

15

# The Central Problem

## A Question of Management

What is wrong with most peoples' lives is the way they are managed. We want to be in control of our own lives and as a result often make a mess of things. Speaking for himself, Paul says that what is wrong is 'the sin that lives in me' (Romans 7:20). The middle letter of 'sin' is 'I'. If we are going to live successfully, we must get rid of the 'I'. A Christian, says Paul, is someone who is able to say, 'It is no longer "I" who live but it is Christ who lives in me' (Galatians 2:20). The difference can be like that of a badly run business which comes under new management. Everything can change for the better. So too we can change if we recognise that Christ is 'the boss'.

## How do you sack the Old Manager?

It is never easy to get rid of sin, the 'I' syndrome in our lives. Sin (the biblical word) is not like a stain that can be removed with detergent—it is more like a cancer that has to be cut out by surgery. Sin reaches into every part of us and dominates all that we do. It even takes away our freedom of choice. 'Everyone who sins is a slave of sin' (John 8:34). This means that 'even though the desire to do good is in me, I am not able to do it' (Romans 7:18). And it gets worse! A small thing like cheating, telling lies, petty stealing can become a big thing and beyond our control. Very quickly a little pet can turn into a wild animal. It is essential that we get rid of this thing before it takes over completely.

## Ask where the Old Manager came from

The Book of Genesis tells us that sin originated with Adam and Eve, the first man and woman. That is why it is sometimes called Original Sin. Adam (= Man) and Eve (= Helper) were allowed by God to eat of any fruit in the Garden of Eden except that which grew on the tree that gave knowledge of what is good and what is bad. Tempted by the serpent (GNB, 'snake'), they decided that they wanted to know everything and ate the forbidden fruit. The whole story is told in Genesis, chapters 2 and 3.

MUSIC

1. Quiz
2. Bible quiz game
3. Bible quiz game
4. God is skethu — Does God exist?

able to trust God.
trusting him with our lives.
Believe in friend

God the Father (Luke 15 11-33)

Joseph tape

# THE BIBLE REVEALS GOD'S PLANS

*Genesis 3:14-21; Romans 8:28;*
*Ephesians 1:3-12*

## WE WANT THE YOUNG PEOPLE TO...

... **explore the idea that God's plans** for salvation, for the future and **for us as individuals are revealed in the pages of the Bible.**

... see that Jesus is the central character in God's master-plan, and that clear clues about Him appear throughout the Old Testament.

## JUST FOR FUN!

# ... and its consequences

The old story says that as soon as Adam and Eve had eaten the forbidden fruit, they knew they had done something wrong. 'They heard the Lord God walking in the garden, and they hid from him among the trees' (Genesis 3:8). This picture language describes so well the effect of sin on our lives. We hide from God.

---

### STORY OF A EWE LAMB

King David wanted to marry the beautiful Bathsheba but she was already married to Uriah. David quietly arranged for Uriah to be killed in a battle. A prophet called Nathan came to David and told him a story about a rich man and a poor man. The rich man had many cattle and sheep but when a visitor called and he wanted to give him a meal, the rich man killed—not one of his own animals—but the single lamb belonging to the poor man. The king said to Nathan, 'That man ought to die for doing such a cruel thing'. The prophet said to the king, 'You are that man! You had everything and you killed Uriah so that you could marry his wife'. At once the king recognised what he had done. 'I have sinned against the Lord,' he said. [Read the whole story in 2 Samuel, chapters 11 and 12]

---

Adam and Eve knew that they had sinned against God but when challenged about it, they began to justify their actions. Adam blamed it on Eve. 'The woman you put here with me gave me the fruit, and I ate it' (Genesis 3:12). Eve in turn blamed the serpent. Our reaction is always to blame someone other than ourselves.

The story ends with Adam and Eve being put out of the garden as a punishment. 'Because of what you have done,' God said to Adam, 'you will have to work hard all your life to make the ground produce enough food for you' (Genesis 3:17). Work, which had been enjoyable while they were still in the garden, now became a sweat.

# This thing called Sin

## Sin is to break any of God's Laws

A biblical word for sin means 'crossing the line'. If you drive through traffic lights when they are at red, you are crossing a line when you should have stopped. That is a sin! God's Laws are lines which are laid down and which must not be crossed.

A good guide to God's Laws are the Ten Commandments (Exodus 20:1–17). We should remember that they are commandments—and not just suggestions! Jesus pointed out that they must be observed in the spirit as well as in the letter. Thus the commandment 'You shall not kill' prohibits also bitterness or hatred which might lead to killing. 'Anyone who [commits murder],' said Jesus in Matthew 5:21–22, 'will be brought to trial; but now I tell you, whoever is angry with his brother will be brought to trial.'

## Sin is to fall short of God's Expectations

Another biblical word for sin means 'missing the mark', a term used in archery. The bull's eye is when we reach 'to the very height of Christ's full stature' (Ephesians 4:13), to match the life and example of Christ in every way. If we fall short of this, we have missed the mark and are committing a sin.

There are both sins of commission and sins of omission. It is as wrong not to help someone in need (sin of omission) as it is to cause someone hurt or harm (sin of commission).

## Sin is to have a broken relationship with God

All sin affects our relationship with God. It is not just a matter of moral failure. The Adam and Eve story is our story. If we go our own way instead of God's way, we create a barrier between us that has to be bridged. Only God can bridge this for us. It was for this that he gave us his Son Jesus.

18

# Jesus is Saviour

God is just and so he cannot tolerate sin. We cannot by ourselves or by our own efforts bridge this broken relationship that our sin has caused. Nothing we do will put us right with God. However, he is willing to forgive us our sin and put right the relationship, because God is also Love. 'Our message is that God was making all mankind his friends through Christ' (2 Corinthians 5:19).

---

### A TALE ABOUT A COURT CASE

Two former schoolfriends met in unusual circumstances. One had become an eminent judge; the other, a notorious criminal. One day the latter found himself in court with his old friend on the bench. He was relieved because he knew that his friend would remember him and let him off lightly. He was wrong. The judge fined him as severely as the law would allow, then he came down into the court, took off his wig and gown, wrote a cheque for the amount and handed it to the clerk. Justice demanded that he should punish his friend for his crime but love for him prompted him to pay the fine himself.

---

We know that Jesus is Saviour . . .

(a) *Because of his Teaching*
He told stories about saving a lost sheep, a lost coin and a lost son. (Read Luke 15:1–32.)

(b) *Because of his Attitude*
He changed unhappy people like Zacchaeus by showing them his friendship. (Read Luke 19:1–10.)

(c) *Because of his Death*
He displayed his love by forgiving even those who had crucified him. (Read Luke 23:34.)

Jesus' Death was Voluntary. He chose to die. 'No-one takes my life away from me. I give it up of my own freewill' (John 10:18).

Jesus' Death was Vicarious (= taking the place of another). Jesus suffered and died for what we did. 'The greatest love a person can have for his friends is to give his life for them' (John 15:13).

**19**

# Jesus is Lord

A creed is a statement of what Christians believe, for example The Apostles' Creed. One of the first Christian creeds was written by St Paul.

> If you confess that Jesus is Lord
> and believe that God raised him from death,
> you will be saved.

(Romans 10:9)

The first Christians saw the resurrection as proof that sin, evil and death no longer had any hold over them. This is why they openly proclaimed that 'Jesus Christ is Lord, to the glory of God the Father' (Philippians 2:11).

## WHY THIS MAN JESUS IS CALLED 'LORD'

Jesus was undoubtedly a good man and a great man but he was more than that. He had an effect on peoples' lives. Nobody could know him and remain unchanged. This is what Mary Magdalene says of him in the musical 'Jesus Christ Superstar':

> I've been changed, really changed.
> In these past few days when I've seen myself,
> I seem like someone else.
> I don't know how to take this.
> I don't see why he moves me.
> He's a man, he's just a man,
> And I've had so many men before . . .

Jesus was a just a man but a man different from all other men. An anonymous writer describes him as a man who had a simple birth and upbringing, who had no credentials but himself and who when he died was laid in a borrowed grave through the pity of a friend. The description ends thus:

> 'Nineteen centuries have come and gone, and today he is the central figure of the human race and the leader of mankind's progress. All the armies that ever marched, all the navies that ever sailed, all the parliaments that ever sat, all the kings that ever reigned, put together, have not affected the life of man on this earth as much as that ONE SOLITARY LIFE.'

This is the man whom Christians address as LORD.

# *This business of being a Christian*

For many people a Christian is simply someone who tries to live according to the teaching of Jesus Christ. Some people who are not particularly religious call themselves Christian—perhaps because they went to Sunday School when they were young or perhaps because they have been brought up in a 'Christian' country. Clearly being a Christian requires more definition than this. Here are two ways of understanding what it means to be a Christian.

## IT IS SOMETHING TO BE BELIEVED

The first part of this book will have given you some idea of what the Christian faith is all about. It is a faith based on the knowledge that God has given us of himself in Jesus Christ. It is summed up in the creed that God is Father, Son and Holy Spirit, and that Jesus Christ is Saviour and Lord. A Christian is someone who understands this and believes it to be true.

## IT IS SOMEONE TO BE RECEIVED

Believing also requires receiving. To receive Christ is to believe that God accepts us as we are with all our shortcomings and failures and does not hold these things against us. 'I will forgive their sins and will no longer remember their wrongs' (Hebrews 8:12).

It is noticeable, however, that Christ never insists on being received. He does not force his way into someone's life. He waits to be invited. 'Listen! I stand at the door and knock; if anyone hears my voice and opens the door, I will come in to his house and eat with him, and he will eat with me' (Revelation 3:20).

In the prologue to St John's Gospel we are reminded that in the beginning Christ 'came to his own country, but his own people did not receive him. Some, however, did receive him . . . so he gave them the right to become God's children' (John 1:11–12). 'All who receive God's abundant grace and are freely put right with him will rule in life through Christ' (Romans 5:17).

21

# *Belonging to Christ and his Church*

## WE BELONG TO CHRIST

Christians are not at liberty to do what they want with their own lives. Their life belongs to God. 'You do not belong to yourselves but to God; he bought you for a price' (1 Corinthians 6:19–20). Jesus, in dying for us on a cross, paid the price for us to be bought back.

There is an old Gospel song that goes thus:

> I belong to Jesus,
>> Jesus belongs to me,
> Not for the years of time alone
>> But for eternity.

If we 'belong to Christ' (1 Corinthians 3:23), then we will see everything around us differently. G W Robinson describes it thus in a hymn:

> Birds with gladder songs o'erflow,
> Flowers with deeper beauties shine,
> Since I know, as now I know,
> I am His, and He is mine.

## WE BELONG TO CHRIST'S CHURCH

The word 'church' comes from a Greek word *kuriakon* (= belonging to the Lord). The Church today is the family of those who belong to the Lord. Peter describes them as 'the chosen race, the king's priests, the holy nation, God's own people' (1 Peter 2:9).

There is an old Glasgow song that goes thus:-

> I belong to Glasgow,
> dear old Glasgow toon.

People are usually proud to belong to a particular city or town or village. Christian people should be similarly proud of belonging to the Church of Jesus Christ.

22

Belonging to Christ means that you belong to his Church. This will be particularly meaningful for you if you are actively involved in the life and work of your local congregation. Many people think that joining a church is like joining a club or an organisation—you pay a subscription and you agree to abide by the rules. Membership of the Church is different. Here are three ways of looking at it.

## BAPTISMAL MEMBERSHIP

Baptism is—and always has been—the sign of entry into the Church (see page 55). In some churches, baptism is only given to those who have made a public profession of their Christian faith. In most churches, baptism is given to the children of those who are already Communicant Members. Anyone who has been baptised, whether of an age to understand it or not, is a Baptised Member of the Church.

## ADHERENT MEMBERSHIP

An Adherent is someone who takes an active part in the life of the Church but does not wish to become a communicant member. Like an adhesive, an adherent is a 'sticker'. In the remoter parts of Scotland, there are many adherents and few communicants. This is often because of their mistaken belief that they are not good enough to become communicant members.

## COMMUNICANT MEMBERSHIP

A Communicant Member is literally someone who has made a Christian commitment as outlined in the vows on page 82 and is thus eligible to receive Communion. It does not depend on the person's worthiness. Sometimes taking this step is referred to as 'joining the Church'. In fact, as has been said, we join the Church when we are baptised, but in the case of those baptised in infancy, this only becomes meaningful when they are of an age to understand what happened at their baptism. Those who have not been baptised in infancy will require to be baptised at the time of joining the Church. Either way, becoming a communicant member confirms what has already taken place at the time of baptism.

# The Church is . . .

The word 'church' can be used in many different senses, for example:

A BUILDING — 'My church is the one with the red spire'
A CONGREGATION — 'She is a member of St Andrew's Church'
A SERVICE — 'Let's all go to church this morning'
A DENOMINATION — 'I belong to the Baptist Church'
AN INSTITUTION — 'The Church should speak out on moral issues'

Let us start with the *church* as a *building*.

Think of the church building that you know best.

How old is it? In what year was it built?

Has it a steeple or a tower—or neither?

Is it rectangular, round or cruciform (= in the shape of a cross)?

The part occupied by the congregation is usually known as the nave. This comes from the Latin *navis* meaning 'a ship'. A ship was one of the early symbols of the Christian Church (see p 31).

The part occupied by the minister and sometimes by the choir is known as the chancel or sanctuary. In old cathedral churches this used to be separated from the nave by a wooden screen.

The Communion Table on which the bread and wine are placed at the Lord's Supper is usually in the chancel area. In some churches it is known as the Altar.

Look also for the Font which holds water for baptisms. In some churches where baptism is by immersion, there is a special baptistry or pool for this purpose. It is covered over when not in use.

Music plays an important part in the worship of most churches. Has your church a pipe organ, an electronic one or a piano? Are other musical instruments ever used? If there is a choir, does it sing any special music, for example an anthem on a Sunday? What hymn book is used? Does it contain modern hymns as well as older hymns?

24

# The People of God

The main meaning of *church* is *people* as Carol Rose Inkeler makes clear in this children's hymn:

> The Church is wherever God's people are praising,
>     Singing their thanks for joy on this day.
> The Church is wherever disciples of Jesus
>     Remember his story and walk in his way.
>
> The Church is wherever God's people are helping,
>     Caring for neighbours in sickness and need.
> The Church is wherever God's people are sharing
>     The words of the Bible in gift and in deed.

Here is what the Bible says about the Church being the People of God.

## The Body of Christ
'All of you are Christ's body, and each one is a part of it' (1 Corinthians 12:27). As a leg or an eye cannot function apart from the body, so neither can we function apart from our fellow Christians. We are Christ's body—his hands, his feet, his ears and his voice.

## The Family in the Faith
(= The Household of God) See Galatians 6:10, NEB. As the Queen personally appoints those who are to belong to the Royal Household, so Jesus appoints those who are to belong to his household or family. 'You did not choose me,' he said, 'I chose you and appointed you' (John 15:16).

## The Flock of God
Jesus talks of his followers as 'one flock with one shepherd' (John 10:16). The Church of the first century appointed leaders 'to be shepherds of the flock that God gave you' (1 Peter 5:2).

## God's Building
Paul refers to the church as 'God's building' and 'Jesus Christ as the one and only foundation' (1 Corinthians 3:9,11). Peter said, 'Come as living stones, and let yourselves be used in building the spiritual temple' (1 Peter 2:5). 'These are the walls of Sparta,' said the king of that ancient city with reference to his bodyguard of soldiers, 'and everyone of them a brick.'

# The Sunday Service

I was glad when they
said to me, Let us go
to the Lord's House
(Psalm 122:1)

The Sunday service should be a joyful occasion—it is the meeting of God's people. The worship of God (= the worth or value we put on God) is the primary task of the Church. We can think of God at any time but at a church service we can focus all our thoughts on him. In worship we are responding to the God who made us, who gave us Jesus Christ and who through him promises to meet with us. 'For where two or three come together in my name,' said Jesus, 'I am there with them' (Matthew 18:20).

## A Congregation is a Family

The ideal congregation should have all generations represented. There should be those in the older age-group who are our link with the past and who can tell us what God has been doing in his Church over the years. There are those in the middle age-group who will provide much of the active membership and who may have special responsibilities as leaders in the congregation. And there are those in the younger age-group—children, teenagers, and so on—who have energy and enthusiasm and often a vision for the future.

## ...in which God is worshipped

We worship God, the Father of the family, as we join in the praise and share in the prayers, the readings, the sermon and the sacraments. It is a good thing, therefore, at the beginning of a service to be quiet for a little while and make ourselves aware of God. 'Be still and know that I am God' (Psalm 46:10, AV).

26

# The Christian Fellowship

Here is a description of life in the first Church in Jerusalem:

> They spent their time in learning from the apostles, taking part
> in the fellowship, and sharing in the fellowship meals and the
> prayers . . . day after day they met as a group in the Temple, and
> they had their meals together in their homes, eating with glad
> and humble hearts, praising God and enjoying the goodwill of
> all the people. And every day the Lord added to their group
> those who were being saved.
>
> (Acts 2:42,46,47)

The fellowship was all important for the first Christians. They
met together, they had meals
together, they prayed together.
It was like living together—not
just meeting for coffee and buns
in the church hall.

## It was a Worshipping Fellowship

At first there were no special buildings for worship so they met in a
part of the Temple in Jerusalem. In your own fellowship, how much
time is spent in worship?

## It was a Learning Fellowship

Its members knew little about the Christian faith and looked to the
apostles for instruction. What about Christian education in your own
church? Is it limited to young people or are adults included?

## It was a Sharing Fellowship

They shared everything—not just their food—but their money and
what they owned (See Acts 4:32–37). The poor especially benefited.
They enjoyed getting a decent meal! How much do we share with our
fellow-Christians?

27

B

# The first thousand years

(circa. AD 35–1000)

The Church as we know it today began with Jesus himself. There had been a Church before that—the Jewish Church—but its structures had become as rigid as dried wineskins. Jesus said that the 'new wine' of his teaching would simply burst through them (see Matthew 9:17). The Church that he began was made up of the twelve disciples (= learners). He trained them to become apostles (= people sent out). Later followers were known as People of the Way.

One of these was Paul who took the Christian message to towns and cities like Antioch and Corinth, and to Rome, the centre of the Roman Empire. The Church in Rome became very strong. Successive Emperors like Nero, afraid that it might become too powerful, persecuted the Christians. This only made them more determined to survive.

In 312 the Emperor Constantine on his way to battle claimed to have seen a cross in the sky and the words, 'By this sign, conquer!' He ordered a cross to be drawn on the shields of his soldiers and he won the battle. From that time he allowed Christians full freedom to worship. Encouraged by the State, the Church in Rome in particular became the most important Church and its Bishop—later called the Pope (= *Papa*, Father)—became leader of the whole Church.

In 330 Constantine made the Greek city of Byzantium the capital of the eastern half of his Empire and re-named it Constantinople—today it is called Istanbul. Soon it rivalled Rome in size and splendour. Christians in the West looked to the Pope as their leader while those in the East looked to the Patriarch of Constantinople.

The Western Church spread from Rome throughout the length and breadth of Europe. Patrick, a Welshman, preached the Gospel in Ireland and became its first bishop in 432. Scotland was evangelised first by Ninian who built his 'little white house' at Whithorn on the Solway Firth in 400, and later by Columba who went from Ireland to Iona in 563 and built an Abbey there. Aidan, a Columbian monk, travelled to the north of England in 634 and built a church on Lindisfarne (Holy Island). By 597 Augustine had brought the Christian Gospel to Canterbury where the Archbishop still has his seat in the cathedral.

28

# The Christian World

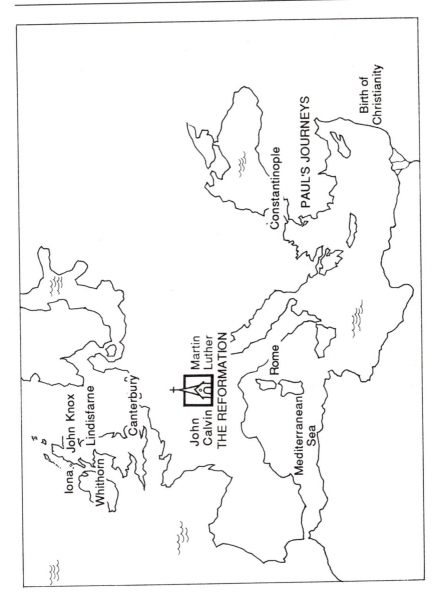

# The second thousand years

(circa. AD 1001–2000)

In 1054 an official split took place between the Eastern and Western Churches. The Church centred in Rome became the [Roman] Catholic Church while the Church centred in Constantinople became the Orthodox (= True) Church.

In 1073 the Roman Church under Hildebrande became the most powerful institution in the West. It also became rich and corrupt. Travelling preachers known as Friars called for a return to the simple Gospel. In 1384 John Wycliffe translated the Bible from Latin into English and sent out bands of preachers to explain the scriptures to the ordinary people.

This was the beginning of the Reformation, a movement which set out to put right many of the wrongs in the Roman Church. In Germany Martin Luther spoke out strongly against the Church's teaching that you could receive a pardon for your sins by paying money to the Church.

Similar protests took place in Switzerland under John Calvin and in Scotland under John Knox. When Mary, Queen of Scots, Defender of the Roman Faith, ordered Mass to be said at Holyrood Palace in Edinburgh, Knox preached against her. The supporters of these protests were called Protestants or Reformers. In England, Henry VIII broke away from the Roman Church for political and personal reasons and called himself 'The Supreme Head of the Church of England'.

The official Church in England was Episcopal (= governed by bishops) but in Scotland it was Presbyterian (= governed by presbyters, otherwise called elders). When, at the Union of 1603, James VI of Scotland became James I of England, he tried to establish Episcopal government in Scotland. Andrew Melville reminded him that though he was King of Scotland, he was not Sovereign of Christ's Realm. The signing of the National Covenant in 1638 established Presbyterianism in Scotland but not before the famous Jenny Geddes had thrown her stool at a minister who dared to use the English Prayer Book in St Giles' Cathedral!

As a result of the Reformation and later Revivals, other branches of the Church developed in Britain, notably Methodists, Congregationalists, Baptists and Brethren. To be more effective in their missionary outreach, many of these Churches got together and in 1910 formed a Council of Churches in Edinburgh. This was the beginning of the World Council of Churches and the Ecumenical Movement—see page 31.

30

# One Church—or many Churches?

There is in fact only one Church—the Church that was 'built upon the foundation laid by the apostles and prophets, the cornerstone being Christ Jesus himself' (Ephesians 2:20). Very early on, however, differences developed within the Church. Paul commented that 'Christ has been divided into groups' (1 Corinthians 1:13).

Today there are major divisions within the Church—the Orthodox, the Roman Catholic, and the Reformed or Protestant Churches. The latter are further divided into separate denominations—Presbyterian, Episcopal, Baptist, Methodist, Congregational, Salvation Army, Pentecostal, Society of Friends (Quakers), and so on. All this gives variety and diversity to the life of the Church, but it also points to a Church that is divided when it should be united.

---

**A SONG FOR UNITY**

We are one in the Spirit,
We are one in the Lord (repeat)
And we pray that all unity may one day be restored.

*Refrain:* And they'll know we are Christians by our love, by our love,
Yes, they'll know we are Christians by our love.

We will walk with each other,
We will walk hand in hand (repeat)
And together we'll spread the news that God is in our land.

*Refrain:* And they'll know we are Christians by our love, by our love,
Yes, they'll know we are Christians by our love.

---

Since 1910 there have been many movements, notably the ECUMENICAL MOVEMENT, to bring the Churches closer together. When Pope John Paul II visited Britain in 1982 he prayed that all Christians might learn to 'walk hand in hand'. The word 'Ecumenical' comes from the Greek *OIKU MENE* ( = the Whole Household). The symbol of the World Council of Churches is the ecumenical ship sailing across the world.

31

# Many Churches within one Church

There are many different churches within the one Church. In some great emphasis is laid on ceremony and ritual, while others hold services that are simple and sometimes quite plain. In some churches the minister or priest plays the major part in leading the worship while in others it is done by lay (= non-clerical) people. Let us look now at some of the mainstream Churches—those which believe in one God, Father, Son and Holy Spirit.

## ROMAN CATHOLIC CHURCH

Historically, this is the oldest Church in the Western world. It is called 'Roman' because it is centred in Rome, but also to distinguish it from other Churches which would call themselves 'catholic'. Catholic, in fact, means 'universal, including all Christians'.

The Roman Catholic Church uses as its basis words spoken by Jesus to Peter, 'You are a rock [the meaning of the word 'Peter'] and on this rock foundation I will build my church' (Matthew 16:18). It believes that Jesus gave Peter special authority to rule the Church. Other Churches would say that Jesus' authority was given—not to Peter as an individual—but to anyone who can make a similar rock-life confession of faith as Peter did when he said, 'You are the Messiah, the Son of the living God' (Matthew 16:16).

Peter is regarded by this Church as being the first Bishop of Rome. The Bishop of Rome came to be called the Pope. The Pope (= *Papa*, Father) lives in the Vatican in Rome. He has as advisers a Council or College of Cardinals. Some priests, honoured by the Pope, are given the title '*Monsignor*'. Friars, Monks and Nuns are members of Religious Orders, for example the Franciscan Order, and they take vows of poverty, chastity and obedience to a Rule.

The Pope is looked upon as Christ's vicar or representative on the earth and his word is authoritative on all matters of Church doctrine and Christian behaviour.

32

# Many Churches within one Church

## EPISCOPAL CHURCH

Episcopal (= *episcop*, bishop) means government by bishops. The Eastern Orthodox, Roman Catholic and Anglican Churches are all episcopal Churches. Anglican Churches are those which follow the tradition of the Church of England where the Archbishop of Canterbury is the leading Bishop. The Church of England is the Established or State-recognised Church in England. In Scotland the Church following the same tradition is called the Scottish Episcopal Church. It is independent of the Church of England and chooses one of its bishops to be the *Primus* or Leading Bishop.

A Cathedral is where the Bishop has his throne or seat (= in Latin, *cathedra*). Other officials of a cathedral are the Dean and Canons. The minister in charge of a cathedral is called the Provost. A Bishop has jurisdiction over an area known as a Diocese and within this are a number of parishes, each under the care of a Rector or Parish Priest. The central act of the Episcopal Church is the Sacrament of Holy Communion or Eucharist (see page 55). The Church uses a Prayer Book which gives readings and prayers for the congregation to join in with.

## METHODIST CHURCH

John and Charles Wesley were two brothers who became clergymen of the Church of England. They felt that the Church at the time was not reaching the ordinary people and in 1729 they and some friends decided to form themselves into a 'holy club' and live their lives *methodically* according to the teaching of the Bible. They met regularly for prayer and study and spent much time visiting the poor and those in prison.

John had an unforgettable religious experience. He felt his heart 'strangely warmed' after visiting a church in Aldersgate in London and soon after the brothers set out on horseback to share with people everywhere a warm-hearted Christian message. John did the preaching while Charles wrote special hymns. 'The world is my parish', said John Wesley; and Methodist preachers today—not all of them are ordained ministers—will go about taking services in many different churches. Normally a Methodist minister will only stay about five years in a particular church.

33

# *Many Churches within one Church*

## PRESBYTERIAN CHURCH

Presbyterianism means government by *presbyters* (= elders). The Church of Scotland is presbyterian and is the national Church in Scotland. At its annual General Assembly the Queen (or her personal representative, the Lord High Commissioner) occupies the Throne Gallery in the Assembly Hall as a symbol of the State's recognition of the Scottish Kirk, as it is called.

The Ministers of a Presbyterian Church are also known as elders— teaching elders as opposed to ruling elders. The Church is governed through a series of courts in the higher of which there is an equal number of elders and ministers. The chairman of each court is known as the Moderator. In the Church of Scotland the supreme court is the General Assembly but below this are Synods (pronounced 'sin-odds'), Presbyteries and Kirk Sessions. The Kirk Session is the court of the local congregation and is made up of the minister and the elders of that particular church.

Presbyterian Churches stress the importance of the scriptures of the Old and New Testaments. Any change in the doctrine of the Church of Scotland, for example, must be 'in agreement with the Word of God'.

There has been a Church in Scotland since the time of Ninian and Columba. Since 1690 the national Church in Scotland has been presbyterian. The symbol of Presbyterianism is the Burning Bush (see Exodus 3:2,3). In 1843 there was a Disruption over the right of congregations to choose their own minister. Many congregations who felt strongly about this came out of the Church of Scotland and formed the Free Church. Most of the Free Church congregations came
together again within the Church of Scotland, but there are still several independent Presbyterian Churches in Scotland including the United Free Church, the Free Church (known as the Wee Frees) and the Free Presbyterian Church.

## UNITED REFORMED CHURCH

This Church which is mainly in England was formed in 1972 and is a union of Presbyterian and Congregational Churches.

**34**

# Many Churches within one Church

## BAPTIST CHURCH
Baptists teach that only those who have a personal faith in Jesus Christ can be baptised. They call this Believers' Baptism. Baptism is generally given by total immersion in water. The Bible is their sole guide to faith. Among well-known Baptists have been John Bunyan, author of *Pilgrim's Progress*, Dr Billy Graham, the world-famous evangelist and Dr Martin Luther King, champion of racial equality.

## CONGREGATIONAL CHURCH
Congregationalists go back to the ways of the early Christians who congregated in each other's houses for worship and Bible reading. Each congregation determines its own form of worship and management. The Pilgrim Fathers who went to America in the 'Mayflower' in 1620 were Congregationalists.

## EVANGELICAL CHURCHES
These are largely groups of Christian lay people (there are no ordained ministers) who form themselves into a Church. They were originally Plymouth Brethren or Christian Brethren. Great stress is laid on the authority of the Bible and the Breaking of Bread (Communion) at the Sunday services. Most Evangelical Churches welcome other Christians although some are less open about this.

## SOCIETY OF FRIENDS (QUAKERS)
This Society was formed in 1624 by George Fox who taught that within everybody's heart God has put an Inner Light (Holy Spirit). At hearing the Word of the Lord, everyone should tremble—hence the name Quaker or Trembler. At Quaker Meeting Houses there is no set pattern for worship and often there is silence until someone is moved to speak.

## SALVATION ARMY
The Army was founded by William Booth, a Methodist minister who tried to bring the Christian faith to the slums of East London. It does much social work among the poor and the needy. The Army is run on military lines with the officers wearing uniform. A special attraction of the Salvation Army are its Bands and Songsters.

35

# The non-Christian Religions

## JUDAISM

Judaism is the religion of the Jews, the chosen people of God. 'I will be your God and you will be my people' (Leviticus 26:12). Jesus was a Jew and so Christianity came out of Judaism. The name 'Judaism' comes from Judah, the land which God promised to Abraham as the home of his people—see Genesis 12:1–3.

In Abraham's time, the Jews were called the Hebrews. Abraham came from the Hebrew tribe. He had a son, Isaac and a grandson, Jacob who was also called Israel. The Hebrews came to be called the Children of Israel or the Israelites. By New Testament times they were called the Jews to distinguish them from the Gentiles (= non-Jews). Here are some things that strict Jews regard as sacred.

### The Holy Books

This usually refers to the first five books of the Bible (in Greek = *Pentateuch*; in Hebrew = *Torah*, meaning Law Books). It includes the Ten Commandments—see Exodus 20:1–17. The Talmud is another Jewish Law Book.

### The Holy Places

The Holy Place was the Temple in Jerusalem, a place of pilgrimage. In each town or village there was a Synagogue (= a Jewish church). Ten male Jews had to be present before a service could be held. The service is led by a rabbi (= a Jewish religious teacher) and the scriptures are in scroll form. Read account of service in Luke 4:16–20.

### The Holy Days

The sabbath is from sunset on Friday to sunset on Saturday. To mark the beginning of it, candles are lit. Men go to synagogue on Friday and the whole family goes on the sabbath (= Saturday, the day of rest). Other Holy Days are Rosh Hushana (New Year) and Yom Kippur (Day of Atonement).

### The Holy Festivals

These are all linked with a harvest—Passover in April (barley), Pentecost in June (wheat), Tabernacles in September (grapes, olives).

36

# The non-Christian Religions

Some non-Christian religions are very old and some are quite modern. Here we have only space to summarise a few of the better-known ones.

## ANCIENT RELIGIONS

**CONFUCIANISM** comes from China. It teaches that human happiness comes from *not* doing to others what you would not want them to do to you.

**BUDDHISM** comes from India. Buddha was a teacher, not a god. Known as 'The Enlightened One', he taught that desire is the cause of suffering. Get rid of desire by following certain moral rules and you will enjoy the blessed peace known as Nirvana.

**HINDUISM** also originated in India and began about 1500 BC. Hindus believe that time is a cycle and that everyone can be re-incarnated in another life in a different form. There is a strict caste or class system with Brahmins at the top and outcastes or untouchables at the bottom.

**ISLAM** is the religion of the Moslems or Muslims. It was founded by Mohammed who was born in Mecca in AD 570. The Moslem Bible is the Koran which contains messages received from God by Mohammed. It tells Moslems that there are five things they must do—recite the creed, pray five times daily, give alms to help the poor, fast during Ramadan (= the month the Koran was given to Mohammed), and make at least one pilgrimage to Mecca. Moslem churches are called Mosques.

## MODERN RELIGIONS

**TRANSCENDENTAL MEDITATION (TM)** was founded by Mahesh Yogi who was born in 1911. His followers must meditate for twenty minutes each morning and evening on a secret phrase which fits their personality.

The **DIVINE LIGHT MISSION** began in 1960 when Guru Ji Maharaj gave 'divine light' to his followers. Every human being has a 'third eye' which can only be opened by the guru who is known as the Perfect Master.

The **HARE KRISHNA MOVEMENT** began in 1965. Their way of life is taught by their guru and its followers wear saffron robes and shave their heads.

# The Cults

There are many religious groups which owe their origin to the Christian Church but which have deviated from it and become separate sects or cults. Some groups, for example Freemasons, have a different origin and claim to be acceptable to people of all religions including Christianity.

## THE UNIFICATION CHURCH (MOONIES)

The nickname comes from the founder, Sun Myung Moon, a Korean who, at the age of sixteen, announced that Jesus had appeared to him and instructed him to restore God's perfect kingdom to the earth. He founded his Church in 1954—not as a separate denomination, but as a movement to save the world. He said that a new Messiah would come who would marry the perfect woman and they would have perfect children. Moon not only founded a Church—he built a multi-million pound network of industries and business links. Moonies sell candles, books and suchlike to help their funds.

## JEHOVAH'S WITNESSES

The name comes from a translation of Isaiah 43:22—'You are my witnesses, says the Lord'. The founder was 'Pastor' Charles Taze Russell who published a new interpretation of the Bible in a magazine called 'The Watchtower'. Jehovah's Witnesses teach that God's Kingdom on earth was established in 1914 and that 'many now living will not see death'. They refuse to take part in religious education classes, to accept blood transfusions, to do military service or to exercise their right to vote. Their churches are called Kingdom Halls.

## CHRISTIAN SCIENTISTS

The Church of Christian Scientists was founded in 1866 by Mary Baker Eddy. It teaches that God is spirit and that he never created matter. Evil things like sin, sickness and death belong to the world of matter and do not exist in God's real world. In her book *Science and Health* with Key to the Scriptures, Mary Baker Eddy says that the cure is to be found in right thinking. This is only given to those who have Christ's Spirit. Their official publication is the 'Christian Science Monitor' and they have special Reading Rooms.

38

# The Cults

## CHURCH OF JESUS CHRIST OF LATTER DAY SAINTS (MORMONS)

The main scripture of this Church is the Book of Mormon which is regarded as a supplement to the Bible. It is a so-called 'translation' of some writing found on golden plates by a man called Joseph Smith (1804–44). To do this work he wore special glasses. Mormons say that God has revealed himself—not just in Jesus Christ—but to Latter Day Saints like Smith himself. They practise Celestial  Marriage and Baptism for the Dead. Headquarters of the Church is in Salt Lake City in Utah. This was built by the Mormons who claimed they had made the desert bloom like a rose. Many young Mormons give two years' missionary service to their Church. They are healthy young people who do not drink alcohol, coffee or tea. Mormons give a tithe (= a tenth) of their income to their Church.

## SEVENTH DAY ADVENTISTS

This group was founded by William Miller (1782–1849) who believed that Christ's Second Coming would be in his own lifetime. The predicted year was 1843 but this passed along with other dates. Now the Church offers no precise date for this Second Advent. Adventists believe that Saturday—the seventh day of the week—should be the day of rest.

## FREEMASONRY

Freemasonry is the largest international secret society in the world. It has strange initiation ceremonies and secret signs and handshakes by which members can recognise each other. It is an all-male friendly society providing help for members in time of need. Its principles are explained as 'brotherly love, relief and truth'. Any believer in God—Christian, Jew, Muslim, Hindu or Buddhist—can become a Freemason. The movement originated during the Middle Ages when all crafts had their secret skills and passwords. One group of craftsmen were the freemasons who travelled freely and helped build cathedrals and churches. Near their place of work they built 'lodges' where they could meet socially, hence the Masonic Lodge today.

# The Occult

We have been looking at the cults—let us now look at the occult. The occult has to do with making contact with the spirit world.

## SPIRITUALISM

Spiritualism is the practice of communicating with the dead through a spirit-help or medium. There is an example of this in 1 Samuel 28:3–19 where the medium employed by Saul was the Witch of Endor.

In its modern form, Spiritualism was founded in 1847 by two sisters, Margaret and Kate Fox. When they were twelve and nine respectively, they heard knocking in their home and decided to get in touch with 'Old Splitfoot', as they called him. They asked him questions and interpreted his answers by the number of raps—one for Yes and two for No. In Spiritualist Churches today, members meet at a seance (= a sitting) and try to communicate with the spirit world.

God warned the Israelites not to consult the spirits of the dead (Deuteronomy 18:11–12). For a Christian, Christ is the only mediator between our world here and the world unseen.

## FORTUNE TELLING

The future belongs to God and we should not concern ourselves with what is going to happen to us. Nevertheless people have always been fascinated about their future and what their fortune is going to be. Crystal gazing is only one way of trying to find out.

The ouija board is another popular method. ('Oui-ja' is a combination of the French and German spellings of the word 'Yes'.) On a table are placed the letters of the alphabet and words like Yes and No. The ouija board has wheels and those taking part sit at the table and place their fingers lightly on top of it. It then 'moves' about the letters of the alphabet and may spell out words which could be the answer to given questions. Tarot cards is another method of fortune telling.

When a slavegirl in Philippi found that she could tell fortunes, her owners made money out of it. Paul said it was an evil spirit that enabled her to predict the future and in the name of Jesus Christ he ordered the spirit to come out of her. Read Acts 16:16–18.

40

# The Occult

## WITCHCRAFT

For most people a witch is a hook-nosed old hag who rides through the night across the face of the moon on a broomstick and is usually associated with Hallowe'en. There is nothing too harmful in this. Black witchcraft or magic, however, can be very dangerous. It can make people do terrible things like sacrificing animals or desecrating Christian symbols. In Ezekiel 13:17,18 we read how the Lord denounces the women who 'sew magic wristbands for everyone and make magic scarves for everyone to wear on their heads, so that they can have power over other peoples' lives'.

## ASTROLOGY

An astrologer is someone who looks at the signs of the Zodiac and tells a person's fortune from the 'star' under which he or she was born. Most people regard the horoscope column in the popular press as being just a bit of fun. Astrology can be dangerous, however, if people begin to plan their lives around what has been predicted.

## LUCKY CHARMS

Many people wear symbols of luck on bracelets or necklaces. These may be quite attractive and are, generally speaking, harmless. As Christians, however, we should remember that life is not a matter of luck—it is all in the plan and purpose of God.

## HYPNOSIS

Hypnosis can provide entertainment but it is also used in psychotherapy, for example to treat diseases like alcoholism or drug addiction. It is potentially dangerous because a hypnotist can make his subject do things of which he or she is not aware. The person can, therefore, come under all kinds of different influences, evil as well as good.

# The Uniqueness of the Christian Faith

It is clear now that there are many other religions and faiths in the world besides Christianity. Some of these have a Christian origin while others embrace features of the Christian religion. Islam, for example, includes Jesus among its prophets. These other religions exist because 'God has always given evidence of his existence by the good things he does' (Acts 14:17). But Christianity claims to have a unique knowledge of God. Although there is much that is good and true in other religions, there is nothing in the world which is good and true which is not also found in Jesus Christ.

If we think of our search to know God in terms of a street plan, we will be confronted by many different paths. Some of these will be blind alleyways. This is inevitable when there are so many concepts of God. Hindus, for example, say that there is not *one* God but *many* gods. Christians claim that Jesus Christ is the only way to a full knowledge and understanding of God.

Jesus said, 'I am the way, the truth and the life; no one goes to the Father except through me' (John 14:6). This claim becomes particularly meaningful when we think of what God has done for us in Jesus Christ. 'Salvation is to be found through him alone; in all the world there is no one else whom God has given who can save us' (Acts 4:12).

The biblical writers were not aware of most of the faiths that we know today. Even before Jesus came, however, they knew that God was a gracious God and that it was possible to know him through faith. 'It was by their faith that people of ancient times won God's approval', but they knew also 'that his purpose was that only in company with us [who are Christians] would they be made perfect' (Hebrews 11:2, 40). All religions are pointers to God, but Christians believe that only in Christ has God made himself known completely.

# Christianity and the other Faiths

## CHRISTIANITY AND OTHER RELIGIONS

Christianity has unique features which are not found in other religions.

### A Belief in God as Father

Apart from Judaism, no other religion claims that God is Father. Buddhists say that God is beyond human knowledge. Hindus say that we can never reach him. Christianity brings God within the grasp of everyone. 'Whoever has seen me,' said Jesus, 'has seen the Father' (John 14:9).

### A Belief that we are God's Children

Christianity teaches that God is willing to accept us as his children while we are 'still sinners' (Romans 5:8). Other religions say that we must first be worthy of God before he will accept us. The Buddhist principle of 'Karma' means that we must pay off our guilt before we can have a right relationship with God.

### A Belief that our Journey on Earth has a Destination

Many religions are like a wheel—there is a cycle of birth, growth, decay and death. Christianity is a journey with a destination. We do not know the route, but we must 'run with determination the race that lies before us...our eyes fixed on Jesus, on whom our faith depends from beginning to end' (Hebrews 12:1,2).


## CHRISTIANITY AND THE CULTS

The Cults or Sects are mostly deviations from mainstream Christianity and its belief in one God, Father, Son and Holy Spirit.

(a) Some claim that they know more about God than Jesus can tell them. According to Paul, however, 'God has already placed Jesus Christ as the one and only foundation' (1 Corinthians 3:11).

(b) Some claim that the Bible has to be supplemented by other scriptures. The Bible alone, says Paul, has 'the wisdom that leads to salvation through faith in Christ Jesus' (2 Timothy 3:15).

(c) Some claim that Jesus is less than God—but it was Jesus who said, 'The Father and I are one' (John 10:30).

43

c

# The Bible—a collection of books

The Bible is not a single book but a collection of 66 books. The word 'Bible' comes from the Greek *biblia* which means 'the little books'. Thirty-nine of the books are in the Old Testament and 27 in the New Testament. The word 'testament' means 'covenant' or 'agreement'. Under the Old Covenant, God made an agreement with the people we know today as the Jews. He promised that he would be their God if they would be his people. The New Covenant is open to everyone who will respond to the love God has shown in Jesus Christ. The books are all listed on page 45.

On a library shelf, these books would be placed under different headings, for example story, history, poetry, prophecy, law, letters, and so on. They are all contained now in one book because they all have this in common—they are describing God's dealings with his people. The whole story of the Bible is outlined on page 48.

There is no one author of the Bible. The books were written over many years by many different people. Some of the earlier stories were first passed down by word of mouth and only years later put into writing. Much, therefore, depended on memory and some parts may have been edited and altered by later writers putting their own interpretation on them.

The books which eventually found their way into the Bible were those which came to be regarded as the most authentic record of God's dealings with his people. They form what is called the Canon of Scripture. ('Canon' means a standard or rule of faith). Some books which were regarded as being less authoritative are called the Apocrypha and are found in some editions of the Bible. (*Apocrypha* = hidden or secret things.)

The books of the Old Testament were the scriptures of the Jewish people and this would be the Bible known to Jesus. The New Testament was a product of the Christian Church and is centred, of course, in the person of Jesus Christ. The four Gospels tell his story and the other books all relate to his purpose in coming into the world.

# The Books of the Bible

**THE OLD TESTAMENT** (originally written in Hebrew)

GENESIS, EXODUS, LEVITICUS, NUMBERS and DEUTERONOMY are known also as the Pentateuch (= Five Books) or the Torah (= Law Books). They contain some history and many of the laws of the Hebrew people.

JOSHUA, JUDGES, RUTH, SAMUEL, KINGS, CHRONICLES, EZRA, NEHEMIAH and ESTHER give an account of the history of Israel and Judah.

JOB, PSALMS, PROVERBS, ECCLESIASTES, SONG OF SONGS and LAMENTATIONS contain poetry, proverbs and philosophy. ISAIAH, JEREMIAH and EZEKIEL are known as the Major Prophets. The Minor Prophets are HOSEA, JOEL, AMOS, OBADIAH, JONAH, MICAH, NAHUM, HABBAKUK, ZEPHANIAH, HAGGAI, ZECHARIAH and MALACHI. The prophets were men sent by God with a special message for his people. DANIEL is a book written to encourage people who were suffering persecution because of their faith.

**THE NEW TESTAMENT** (originally written in Greek)

MATTHEW, MARK, LUKE and JOHN are the four Gospels. 'Gospel' means good news, glad tidings—in Chinese idiom, happy sound. They tell 'the Good News about Jesus Christ, the Son of God' (Mark 1:1).

ACTS was written by Luke and tells about the Acts of the Apostles and of some of the leaders in the early Church.

Paul wrote many letters (sometimes referred to as epistles) to the churches he started—ROMANS, CORINTHIANS, GALATIANS, EPHESIANS, PHILIPPIANS, COLOSSIANS and THESSALONIANS— and to individual Christians—TIMOTHY, TITUS and PHILEMON. JAMES, PETER, JUDE and JOHN also wrote letters. The author of the Letter to the HEBREWS is unknown.

REVELATION was written by a man called John who, because he was a Christian, was exiled to an island in the Mediterranean. The book is full of visions which he claimed to have received from God in a revelation and which he put into writing to encourage Christians who were being persecuted.

# How the Bible came to be written

The earliest stories in the Bible were passed down by word of mouth. When trading began between nations, there arose the need for writing. It was first in the form of pictures, then of letters.

The Bible was originally written on papyrus, a kind of paper produced from the pith of the papyrus reeds which grew by the banks of rivers. The writing was done in solid columns on long sheets which were then rolled up and called 'scrolls'. Later they were produced in book form and were known as 'codices'.

In 1947 a Bedouin shepherd boy came across a collection of scrolls in stone jars in a cave near the Dead Sea. These turned out to be some of the oldest manuscripts that we have of the Bible and they are known as the Dead Sea Scrolls. They can be seen in the Shrine of the Book at the Israel Museum in Jerusalem.

By the time of Christ, Hebrew was the written language of the Jews although the spoken language tended to be Aramaic. There are some phrases of this preserved in the Bible. When Jesus said from the cross, 'Eli, Eli, lema sabachthani?' (= 'My God, my God, why did you abandon me?') (Matthew 27:46), he was speaking Aramaic. Hebrew is written from right to left. The words are sometimes not separated from each other and the vowels are indicated by various dots and strokes. Below are the first words of the Bible—'IN THE BEGINNING'—in Hebrew and then in Greek, the language of the New Testament.

בְּרֵאשִׁית        'Ἐν ἀρχῇ

Much of the New Testament was not written down until long after Jesus' day. This was because people believed that he would shortly return and there would be no need to put anything into writing. The earliest Gospel—that of Mark—was not written until around AD 60. The oldest writing in the New Testament is Paul's Letter to the Thessalonians which is dated around AD 50.

# ... and the story of its translation

One of the earliest translations of the Bible was a Greek version of the Old Testament in 270 BC. It was called the SEPTUAGINT (= Seventy) because seventy scholars had worked on it. In AD 385, St Jerome translated the whole Bible into Latin. This was called the VULGATE (= popular edition). At first all Bibles were written out by hand, mainly by monks.

Latin was only understood by the priests and so in 1342 John Wycliffe translated the Bible into English. This opened it up to ordinary people. 'To be ignorant of the Scriptures,' he said, 'is to be ignorant of Christ.' With the invention of printing, many more Bibles became available. This seemed to the priests to be taking away their control of the Scripture and they put up much opposition to it. When William Tyndale tried to print Bibles in English, the Church of England condemned him and he had to finish his work on the Continent. In 1536 Tyndale was burned at the stake for translating the Bible.

Today the Bible has been translated into thousands of languages through the work of the Bible Societies. Their aim is to provide everyone with a Bible in a language that they can understand and at a price that they can afford to pay.

## USEFUL TRANSLATIONS OF THE BIBLE

Some people still like to use the AUTHORISED VERSION (AV), also known as the KING JAMES VERSION (KJV) because it was published on the authority of King James I of England (James VI of Scotland) in 1611. It contains words and phrases that will not be familiar to many modern readers. A more up-to-date version which retains the style— but not the language—of the Authorised Version is the REVISED STANDARD VERSION (RSV) which came out in 1952.

Of the modern translations of the Bible, an official publication of all the main Churches is the REVISED ENGLISH BIBLE (REB). More popular versions are the GOOD NEWS BIBLE (GNB) and the NEW INTERNATIONAL VERSION (NIV). The LIVING BIBLE (LB) gives a useful paraphrase rather than a translation of the original text.

# The Story of the Bible

## THE OLD TESTAMENT

The first book, **GENESIS**, tells about the creation or origin of all things and of how the first man and woman (Adam and Eve) were put out of the Garden of Eden because they had disobeyed God. God then made a series of covenants including one with Noah in which he promised that he would never again destroy the whole of mankind with a flood.

Later God made a covenant with Abraham who came from Ur near the Persian Gulf. He said that he would make him the founder of a great nation and would give his people a special country in which to live. This Promised Land was the land of Canaan—today it is called Israel. Abraham's descendants (the Twelve Tribes of Israel) were called the Israelites. We know them today as the Jews.

One of Jacob's sons, Joseph, was banished by his brothers to Egypt but later, during a time of famine, they were reconciled and the family went to live in Egypt. A later Pharaoh (= King of Egypt) made the Israelites into slaves but God rescued them through Moses. After forty years in the wilderness, he brought them back to the land God had originally given them. The whole story is told in the Book of **EXODUS**.

In Canaan they were ruled first by **JUDGES** and then by **KINGS**. The most famous King was David. He was succeeded by his son, Solomon, who also built the first Temple in Jerusalem. After Solomon, the country was split between a Northern Kingdom and a Southern Kingdom. Eventually both Kingdoms collapsed and many of the Israelites were taken into exile in Babylon. Jerusalem (also known as Zion) became their focalpoint during the exile and they longed to return there. When eventually they did, they were always subject to another power.

## THE NEW TESTAMENT

When Jesus was born, a Roman government was in power in Israel. The **GOSPELS** tell his life story with an account also of his death, his resurrection and his ascension. The Book of **ACTS** gives an account of the beginnings of the Christian Church. Then follows a series of letters to various churches and individual Christians.

**48**

# The World in Biblical times

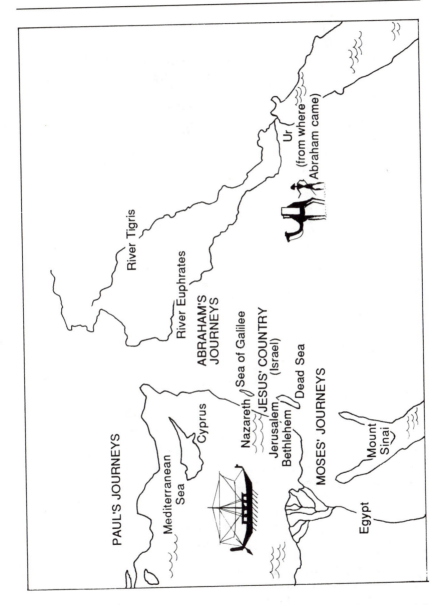

# How to go about reading the Bible

READ

A PAGE A DAY

The Bible is not like an ordinary book where you start at the beginning and continue to the end. As has been said, it is made up of many books. If you would like to read the Bible right through in a modern version, get a copy of the **ONE YEAR BIBLE**. The entire Bible has been arranged in 365 readings with a daily section from the Old Testament, the New Testament, a few verses from a Psalm and a Proverb.

If you can spend some time on it, the **DAILY STUDY BIBLE** series begun by Dr William Barclay provides a clear, short commentary on every book in the Bible. If you have limited time, try one of the Bible reading schemes published by the Bible Reading Fellowship, the International Bible Reading Association, the Scripture Union or the Salvation Army. Some of these are graded for different age groups. All such study aids should be obtainable from Church or Christian bookshops.

## GETTING DOWN TO IT

The Bible may be read alone or along with others. If there is a Bible Study or Housegroup where you live, it could be helpful to you to join it. Don't feel you have to be specially knowledgeable about the Bible before you join such a group. We are all learning together!

If you are reading the Bible on your own, be businesslike about it. Don't just start reading as you are nodding off to sleep! Discipleship means self-discipline. Try to set apart ten minutes each day for reading the Bible. You may soon want to extend that period. Remember it is God's Word and that he can 'speak' to you through it as you read and try to understand what it is saying.

\* \* \*

There follow now three stories from St Luke's Gospel. Read them in turn along with the background notes and then ask yourselves the suggested questions. This is a simple way of studying the Bible.

# A look at St Luke's Gospel—Neighbours

The teacher of the Law asked Jesus, 'Who is my neighbour?'

Jesus answered, 'There was once a man who was going down from Jerusalem to Jericho when robbers attacked him, stripped him and beat him, leaving him half dead.

'It so happened that a priest was going down that road, but when he saw the man, he walked on, on the other side. In the same way a Levite also came along, went over and looked at the man, and then walked on by, on the other side.

'But a Samaritan who was travelling that way came upon the man, and when he saw him, his heart was filled with pity. He went over to him, poured oil and wine on his wounds and bandaged them; then he put the man on his own animal and took him to an inn, where he took care of him. The next day he took out two silver coins and gave them to the inn-keeper. "Take care of him," he told the inn-keeper, "and when I come back this way, I will pay you whatever else you spend on him."'

Jesus concluded, 'In your opinion, which of these three acted like a neighbour towards the man attacked by the robbers? The teacher of the Law said, 'The one who was kind to him!' Jesus replied, 'You go, then, and do the same'.

LUKE 10:29–37

---

### NOTES

The priest and the Levite would both be employed at the Temple in Jerusalem. Touching a dead body (if the man was dead) would debar them from going into the Temple. The Samaritan must have been a regular traveller who stayed at this inn. Presumably the wounded man was a Jew and normally Samaritans would have nothing to do with Jews. Two silver coins would be the equivalent of a day's wage.

---

(1) What would you do if you saw someone, possibly dead, lying at the side of the road?

(2) The Samaritan not only gave the man First Aid; he paid the inn-keeper to look after him. How far do we go in helping a neighbour?

## 51

D

# A look at St Luke's Gospel—Worry

Jesus said to his disciples, 'And so I tell you not to worry about the food you need to stay alive or about the clothes you need for your body. Life is much more important than food, and the body much more important than clothes.

'Look at the crows; they don't sow seed or gather a harvest; they don't have store-rooms or barns; God feeds them! You are worth more than the birds! Can any of you live a bit longer by worrying about it? If you can't manage even such a small thing, why worry about the other things? Look how the wild flowers grow; they don't work or make clothes for themselves. But I tell you that not even King Solomon with all his wealth had clothes as beautiful as one of these flowers. It is God who clothes the wild grass—grass that is here today and gone tomorrow, burnt up in the oven. Won't he be all the more sure to clothe you? How little faith you have!

'So don't be all upset, always concerned about what you will eat and drink. (For the pagans of this world are concerned about all these things.) Your Father knows that you need these things. Instead, be concerned with his Kingdom, and he will provide you with these things.'

LUKE 12:22–31

---

**NOTES**

Peoples' worries then were largely financial. Taxation was high. Wealth was often in the form of expensive clothes. The wild flowers (AV, 'lilies of the field') were scarlet anemones. They were used as fuel for a fire as wood was scarce.

---

(1) Do you ever worry about how you are going to manage financially? How important to you are things like food and clothes? If your house were to go on fire, what 'things' would you want to save?

(2) Does Jesus mean that we shouldn't worry at all about the future?

(3) Can you think of ways in which your lifestyle might be simpler? What is meant by saying, 'Live simply that others may simply live'?

52

# A look at St Luke's Gospel—Prayer

Jesus said to his disciples, 'Suppose one of you should go to a friend's house at midnight and say to him, "Friend, let me borrow three loaves of bread. A friend of mine who is on a journey has just come to my house, and I haven't got any food for him!" And suppose your friend should answer from inside, "Don't bother me! The door is already locked, and my children and I are in bed. I can't get up and give you anything". Well, what then? I tell you that even if he will not get up and give you the bread because you are his friend, yet he will get up and give you everything you need because you are not ashamed to keep on asking.

'And so I say to you, "Ask, and you will receive; seek, and you will find; knock, and the door will be opened to you. For everyone who asks will receive, and he who seeks will find, and the door will be opened to anyone who knocks. Would any of you who are fathers give your son a snake when he asks for a fish? Or would you give him a scorpion if he asks for an egg? Bad as you are, you know how to give good things to your children. How much more then will the Father in heaven give the Holy Spirit to those who ask him?'

LUKE 11:5–13

---

### NOTES

This story follows and in part explains the Lord's Prayer which you will find at the beginning of this chapter. It was not unusual for travellers to be late on the road—in the East, it is too hot to travel during the day. Also hospitality was a sacred duty. There may have been no bread in the house because bread was normally made fresh each day and not kept over. If a house door was locked—the door was usually left open during the day—it meant that the occupants had gone to bed and didn't want to be disturbed. Everyone slept close together on the floor to keep warm. If one got up, everyone was liable to wake.

---

(1) Was Jesus saying in this story that God is like the householder who wouldn't get up to open the door?

(2) Is this story telling us that if we go on asking long enough, we will get what we ask for? Does it tell us anything about prayers that don't seem to get answered?

(3) In what ways is this story an explanation of the Lord's Prayer?

53

# The Word and Sacrament

## GOD'S WORD

We have been looking at the **BIBLE**. This is often referred to as the Word of God. It was what certain people believed God was saying to them from their experience of the world at that time.

 It was not that God dictated words to them and they wrote them down; rather he inspired them—not in the sense that he gave them bright ideas, but he 'breathed' into their thoughts and their imagination and their understanding of the world. 'All scripture is inspired by God' (2 Timothy 3:16).

What they wrote down was God's Word for them and it has become God's Word for us also. The same God who inspired the original writers speaks to us through them. As we read and study their words, so they become God's Word for us today.

## GOD'S SACRAMENTS

 We are now going on to look at **BAPTISM** and **COMMUNION**, the Sacraments of the Church. As God speaks through the Bible, so he speaks also through the Sacraments. A sixteenth century minister, Robert Bruce wrote, 'We get no other thing nor no new thing in the Sacrament but the same thing which we get in the Word, but we get that same thing better'.

What is a Sacrament? It is a special way in which God speaks to people through something visible and tangible. We can convey sympathy or good wishes to someone by using words, but we can do it much more meaningfully by giving flowers or by putting our arm around the person. In the same way, we can tell people about God's goodness and love using just words but we can say the same thing with much greater effect through the Sacraments. Let us now look at them in greater detail.

54

# Baptism and Communion

Quakers and the Salvation Army do not observe Sacraments. Roman Catholics have seven Sacraments—the Sacraments of Baptism, Confirmation, Communion, Holy Orders, Marriage, Penance and the Sick. Most Churches observe only the Sacraments for which there is a warrant in the New Testament, namely Baptism and Communion.

## BAPTISM

> Jesus said, 'Go to all peoples everywhere and make them my disciples, baptise them...'
>
> (Matthew 28:19)

Baptism is the Sacrament of initiation or introduction into the Church. Those who come into the Christian fellowship must first be 'washed clean' in a spiritual sense. That is why water is used as a symbol. Some Churches practise Believers' Baptism: only those who acknowledge Jesus Christ as Saviour and Lord can be baptised. In other Churches, Baptism is given to infants. Depending on the circumstances, Baptism can be by immersion in water, or more usually by water being sprinkled or poured over the forehead. Being an initiation Sacrament, it can only be given once.

## COMMUNION

> Jesus said, 'This is my body, which is for you; do this in memory of me...'
>
> (1 Corinthians 11:24)

The Sacrament of Communion recalls the Last Supper that Jesus had with his disciples. The only elements of the original meal still used are the bread and the wine. These symbolise Christ's body and blood. In some Churches there is Communion every Sunday; in others, only occasionally. Communicants either go to the Communion Table or Altar to receive Communion, or the bread and wine are brought to them in their seats.

The Sacrament is given different names by different Churches, for example Communion, the Lord's Supper, the Eucharist (= the Thanksgiving), or the Breaking of Bread. Roman Catholics refer to it as the Mass.

55

# What Baptism means

The meaning and effect of Baptism is the same at whatever age it takes place. In the case of Infant Baptism, however, it will only mean something to the person concerned when he or she is old enough to understand. Here are three important aspects of Baptism.

## The Forgiveness of Sins

John the Baptist said, 'Turn away from your sins and be baptised and God will forgive your sins' (Luke 3:3). Jesus who 'was without sin' (2 Corinthians 5:21) wanted to identify himself with everyone—with sinful people like ourselves. That is why he asked John to baptise him. He then went on to pay the penalty for all our sins by allowing himself to be put to death on a cross. Baptism thus becomes a sign that we have been forgiven (= washed clean of all sin) because of what Christ has done.

## The Gift of the Holy Spirit

When Jesus was baptised by John, 'he saw the Spirit of God coming down like a dove and alighting on him' (Matthew 3:16–17). In Baptism, God's Holy Spirit is given. On the Day of Pentecost, Peter said to the people, 'Each of you must turn away from his sins and be baptised in the name of Jesus Christ so that your sins will be forgiven you, and you will receive God's gift, the Holy Spirit' (Acts 2:38). This gift is the power that God gives people to enable them to live a new life in Christ.

## The New Life in Christ

Baptism is a sign that this new life can now begin. As Jesus died and rose again, so 'by our baptism [in water], we were buried with him and share his death, in order that, just as Christ was raised from death . . . so also we might live a new life' (Romans 6:4). In the early Church, the beginning of this new life was symbolised by a ceremony on the Day of Pentecost when those who had been baptised in the river came out of the water and put on clean white robes—hence the modern White or Whit Sunday.

56

# ... and why babies are Baptised

Many Churches practise what is called Infant Baptism. Sometimes it is referred to as a Christening. Originally only those who were Christian believers wanted to be baptised. Gradually, however, whole households were being baptised and this must have included children. What it required was that the head of the family be a believer. 'Believe in the Lord Jesus', Paul said to the gaoler in Philippi 'and you will be saved, you and your family... and he and all his family were baptised at once' (Acts 16:31,33). Today, infants can be baptised if a parent or someone responsible is a believer and will promise to give the child a Christian upbringing.

The idea of Infant Baptism is found in the Old Testament where God made a covenant with Abraham and said, 'I will be your God and the God of your descendants' (Genesis 17:7). As a sign of this, every baby boy of eight days old had to be circumcised (= a slight operation on the foreskin). It was a permanent reminder to the person that he was one of God's chosen people. In the same way, Baptism is a sign of the new covenant which God made with his people through Jesus Christ. 'God's promise', said Peter, 'was made to you and your children' (Acts 2:39).

## What actually happens in Infant Baptism

Infant Baptism is not like an inoculation to give immunity against sin! There is no guarantee that a baptised baby will grow up and be spiritually healthy! Baptism is simply God's chosen way to introduce us to the life of faith. Through it a child is grafted into Christ 'as a wild olive can be grafted... into a cultivated olive' (Romans 11:24, RSV). Given a Christian upbringing, the child will hopefully 'grow up in every way to Christ' (Ephesians 4:15). Behind Infant Baptism is the intention that the child should grow up in the faith to the point where he or she can make it a personal faith and thus confirm the vows that were taken at the time of his or her Baptism.

57

# What Communion means

Here are some of the ways in which we can think of the Lord's Supper:

## As a Commemorative Meal

> Jesus said, 'Do this in memory of me.'
>
> (1 Corinthians 11:24)

In this way we are remembering the man Jesus and the life he lived on this earth. The bread and the wine symbolise Jesus' body and blood and so help us to remember that he was once a man of flesh. In the breaking of bread, however, we are also reminded of his death and of the sacrifice he made for us when he was crucified. 'The greatest love a person can have for his friends is to give his life for them' (John 15:13). This Sacrament helps us to remember Jesus.

---

**A LEGEND ABOUT ZACCHAEUS**

It is told that after his conversion, Zacchaeus would sometimes vanish and no-one would know where he had gone. One day some of his new friends watched him and followed him to a spot beneath a sycamore tree. 'Why do you come here?' they asked him. 'It was from this tree,' said Zacchaeus, 'that I first saw Jesus. Whenever I get tempted to go back to my old way of life, I come out and stand beneath this tree and remember him where I first saw him. When I do that, the temptation goes.'

---

## As a Communion Meal

> Jesus said, 'Whoever eats my flesh and drinks my blood lives in me, and I live in him'.
>
> (John 6:56)

Jesus cannot have meant us to take these words literally. At the last supper, Jesus held a piece of bread in his hand and said, 'This is my body'. It wasn't actually his body for he was still standing there in the flesh. In no sense are we literally eating flesh or drinking blood. That is where this understanding of the Sacrament can be helpful. In this

58

# What Communion means

Sacrament we are symbolically taking Christ into our lives—'flesh and blood', as it were—and in that sense we are having communion with him.

## As a Fellowship Meal

'They spent their time . . . sharing in the fellowship meals.'
(Acts 2:42)

For the first Christians the Sacrament was almost certainly a part of a family meal or a meal with fellow Christians in a private house. It was often known as the *Agape* or Love Feast. It provided not only food but fellowship. The Sacrament today is not a proper meal—only a morsel of bread (in some churches called a wafer) and a sip of wine are used—but the element of fellowship is still an essential part of it. At the Lord's Table we are a family invited to share in a meal.

## As a Thanksgiving Meal

'Jesus took a cup, gave thanks to God, and handed it to them.'
(Mark 14:23)

Some Churches call this definition of the Sacrament the 'Eucharist'. This comes from a Greek word meaning 'to give thanks'. At the Lord's Supper we are particularly thankful for the gift of Jesus Christ. It should, therefore, never be a solemn occasion but a time to rejoice and be glad.

'This is the hour of banquet and of song,
This is the heavenly table spread for me;
Here let me feast, and feasting, still prolong
The hallowed hour of fellowship with thee.'
(Horatius Bonar)

## As a Proclamation Meal

'Every time you eat this bread and drink from this cup you proclaim the Lord's death until he comes.'
(1 Corinthians 11:26)

A feature of the early Christian faith was the belief that Jesus would one day return 'in his glory' (Luke 9:26). When that day comes, there will be no need for any further celebration of the Sacrament. Until then, however, we must continue to observe it and in doing so, proclaim to the world what Christ did for us and for all people when he died on the cross.

59

# Communion—where it all started

Jesus had a last supper with his disciples in an upstairs room in a house in Jerusalem. This supper was to celebrate the Jewish Passover. 'Jesus sent off Peter and John with these instructions, "Go and get the Passover meal ready for us to eat"' (Luke 22:8). Normally the Passover was celebrated by families in their own homes. Jesus' 'family' at the time were his twelve disciples and so he arranged with a friend to keep the Passover in his house in Jerusalem. A man carrying a water jug (normally only women carried water jugs) would show Peter and John where the house was. There in 'the upper room' they prepared the meal.

---

### KEEPING THE PASSOVER

When God sent Moses to bring the Israelites out of Egypt (see Exodus 11ff), the Pharaoh (King of Egypt) would not let them go. As a punishment God said, 'Every first-born son in Egypt will die, from the king's son...to the son of the prisoner in the dungeon' (Exodus 11:5; 12:29). The only exceptions would be the families of the Israelites. They were to mark their houses by killing a lamb, smearing its blood on the top and sides of their doors and then, before leaving, have a hurried meal of lamb, unleavened bread (there would be no time to put leaven or yeast in it) and bitter herbs (a reminder of bitter times in Egypt). That night death came to every family in Egypt but passed over (PASSOVER) the homes of the Israelites. Since then their descendants have kept the Passover as a reminder of what God did that night to save them.

---

That night as Jesus celebrated this Passover with his disciples, he changed its meaning and applied it to himself. 'As he broke the bread, he said, "This is my body, which is for you. Do this in memory of me". In the same way he gave the cup after the supper saying, "This cup is God's new covenant sealed with my blood. Whenever you drink it do so in memory of me"' (1 Corinthians 11:23–25). Jesus was demonstrating that by his death on a cross, the death that we should have suffered has 'passed over' us.

60

# What Prayer is

 Many people's idea of prayer goes back to their childhood days. Prayer for them has to do with asking for things and God is seen as a kind of Father Christmas who gives us what we ask for. But is this really what prayer is about? Here are some thoughts on prayer.

## PRAYER IS ABOUT FINDING TIME FOR GOD

Before we can pray at all, we must find time to pray. For most of us, prayer is not a priority. There are so many other things we have to do—or want to do—that prayer simply gets crowded out. To pray, it is necessary first to make an appointment with God, to find a time when we can sit (or kneel) quietly and know that he is there. Remember that God 'is near to those who call to him' (Psalm 145:18).

Some people find it helpful to read some verses from the Bible before they pray. This may mean having a special place for prayer. Edward Wilson, who sailed with Captain Scott on his journey to the South Pole, used the crow's nest of the ship as what he called 'my private chapel'. Jesus said, 'When you pray, go to your room, close the door and pray to your Father, who is unseen' (Matthew 6:6). The room may be a room in your house or a compartment in your mind where you can shut out other things and think of God—but find time to go into that room.

## PRAYER IS ABOUT WASTING TIME WITH GOD

There are those who say that praying is a waste of time. In a very real sense, prayer could be described as 'wasting time with God'. When we are able to relax completely with God present, then time doesn't matter. We are like two close friends. They are not speaking to each other all the time. They just enjoy being together. Prayer is simply being in the company of God. St Teresa once said, 'The life of prayer is just love to God, and the custom of being ever with him'. When we have that kind of relationship with God, then it doesn't matter whether we talk with him or are silent. Being with him is all that matters.

**61**

# Making a start with Prayer

There is an African proverb that says—If you want to climb a tree, start at the bottom and not at the top. Prayer sometimes feels like climbing a tree. God seems to be up at the top of the tree and we are at the bottom. When we start to climb, however, we never reach God. He is always beyond us. The only way we can meet with him is if he comes down to where we are. This is exactly what he does in Jesus Christ.

There is a hymn by Oliver Wendell Holmes that describes very well—both in the words and in the music—how God comes to meet with us. The words of the first verse picture God 'throned afar' and way beyond our human reach. In the last line, however, God is depicted as coming close 'to each loving heart':

> Lord of all being, throned afar,
> Thy glory flames from sun and star;
> Centre and soul of every sphere,
> Yet to each loving heart how near!

Similarly, the first three lines of the music are like man's effort to reach God. Each phrase brings us a bit nearer but each time we have to turn back without getting there. In the final bars, the music matches the words of the final line of the hymn—God comes down to meet with us where we are.

Before we pray, it is a good thing to think of God 'up there' in all his greatness and majesty and power. 'Think magnificently about God,' wrote Sir Thomas Browne, a seventeenth century English author. We can then go on to think of that same God as the Father who comes close to each one of us in Jesus Christ.

62

# ... and where we go from there

If we have been able to make ourselves 'aware of the Lord's presence' (Psalm 16:8) in the ways suggested, we can then go on to think of prayer in a number of different ways.

## THANKSGIVING
Someone once said, 'The thankful heart is the only door that opens to God'. To be able to give thanks to God is to acknowledge that he is the bountiful Giver. 'He gave us his son,' Paul says in Romans 8:32, 'will he not freely give us all things?' We must be able to thank God for everything, for the bad things as well as for the good things. Disappointments can be blessings in disguise and bitter experiences are often a way to a better understanding of God.

## CONFESSION
Confession, said Martin Luther once, is punishment time. We don't like confessing the weaknesses in our life because it hurts our pride. Confession, however, is necessary if we are going to have any kind of real relationship with God. 'If we confess our sins to God, he will forgive us our sins and purify us from all our wrongdoing' (1 John 1:9). It always clears the conscience to make a clean breast of things. When we pray, there must be no barrier between ourselves and God.

## SUPPLICATION
Supplication means asking for things. 'Ask, and you will receive,' said Jesus in Matthew 7:7. This means, not so much asking for what we want, as trying to discover what God wants for us. Jesus' own prayer was, 'Not what I want, but what you want' (Matthew 26:39). We must always work on the assumption that God knows what we need and what we ought to ask for.

## INTERCESSION
Intercession means praying for other people. Paul said, 'I urge that petitions, prayers, requests and thanksgivings be offered to God for all people' (1 Timothy 2:1). Start where you are by praying for the people in your immediate circle and then widen the circle until you are including people all over the world. Remember that no-one anywhere is more than a prayer away.

63

# Praying—some hints

Here are some things that are worth keeping in mind when you pray.

## Be Detailed in your Prayers

God is interested in detail. He knows everything about us. 'Even the hairs of your head have all been counted,' said Jesus (Matthew 10:30). If a thing is important to you, then no matter how small or trivial it is, it is important to God and you can speak to him about it.

## Be Expectant in your Prayers

Have you ever prayed for something to happen—and it doesn't? Then did you expect something to happen? It is no use praying for a miracle if you don't believe a miracle is possible. God is a great God and we should never limit his powers. To a man who brought his epileptic son for him to heal, Jesus said, 'Everything is possible for the person who has faith' (Mark 9:23). And he healed the man's son. Expect great things of God.

## Be Persistent in your Prayers

Jesus tells a story about a widow who took her case to court—see Luke 18:1–8. 'Help me against my opponent,' she said. Judges in these days would often act only if they were bribed. This judge would take no action to help the woman because she had no money. She went on pleading with him until eventually he agreed to help her. Clearly God is not like this judge but the story is told to illustrate the need for persistence in prayer. God has to know how much we want his help. If we really want something, we will not just knock once but go on knocking.

## Be Resigned in your Prayers

If you pray earnestly for something and you don't get it, accept that this may be God saying 'It's not for you!' Paul had a painful ailment and he prayed three times for it to be taken away. It didn't go away. God's reply was, 'My grace is all you need' (2 Corinthians 12:9). We may not get what we ask for in our prayers but God will help us to cope with our situation whatever it is.

# The Lord's Prayer

Jesus gave his disciples a prayer which was to be the pattern for all prayer. We call it the Lord's Prayer. Below is printed the version found in Matthew 6:9–13.

**OUR FATHER, WHICH ART IN HEAVEN, HALLOWED BE THY NAME**
'Father' was Jesus' special name for God. By saying 'Our Father', we are acknowledging the fact that we are a Christian family praying together. 'Heaven' describes where God is. 'Hallowed' means 'to be treated as holy'.

**THY KINGDOM COME, THY WILL BE DONE, ON EARTH AS IT IS IN HEAVEN**
The Kingdom of God is where God's rule is observed and his will is done. We are to pray for the coming of that Kingdom in our own world here. It must start, of course, in our own lives. There is an old Negro prayer that says, 'Bring in the Kingdom, Lord, and begin it with me'.

**GIVE US THIS DAY OUR DAILY BREAD**
In Jesus' time, bread had to be baked each day. We are asking God to look after us in the day immediately ahead of us only. Note that this prayer is for bread, not for cake; for the necessities, not for luxuries.

**FORGIVE US OUR DEBTS AS WE FOR- GIVE OUR DEBTORS**
'Give' is followed by 'forgive'. According to the story in Matthew 18:23–35, God will only forgive us if we are forgiving towards others. 'Debts' implies that we owe God something. 'Trespasses' in the alternative version of the Prayer has to do with crossing forbidden lines.

**AND LEAD US NOT INTO TEMPTATION BUT DELIVER US FROM EVIL**
The word 'temptation' always suggests that there is something evil around the corner. The word should really be translated 'testing'. The NEB offers, 'Do not bring us to the test but save us from the evil one'. In Jesus' day in particular, people believed in a personal devil who tested their human endurance.

**FOR THINE IS THE KINGDOM, THE POWER AND THE GLORY, FOR EVER.**

This is the doxology (= hymn of glory) which is not found in the original prayer but is a fitting way to conclude it.

# How long have we got?

The clock is a reminder that time is never on our side. Jesus said, 'A day has twelve hours, hasn't it?' (John 11:9). There is only so much we can do each day but God means us to use our time wisely and well. 'As long as it is day,' said Jesus, 'we must keep on doing the work of him who sent me; night is coming when no-one can work' (John 9:4).

'THERE IS A TIME FOR EVERY MATTER UNDER HEAVEN.'

(Ecclesiastes 3:1, RSV)

### A Fact we cannot disregard

No-one knows exactly how long he or she will live. The Bible says, 'Seventy years is all we have . . . eighty years, if we are strong' (Psalm 90:10). The number of years is not the important thing. The important thing, says Paul, is to 'be careful how you live . . . make good use of every opportunity you have' (Ephesians 5:15,16). By doing this, some people can live as full a life in thirty years as others will do in twice that time.

### . . . and some Questions to ask ourselves

Am I making the best use of my time?

Am I using each day in the way a Christian should? Do I sometimes fritter my time away or am I always looking at my watch and wondering if I can get everything done?

Do I give long enough to God in prayer or in reading my Bible? Do I give enough time to my family and people who need me? Do I sometimes overwork? Or do I sometimes spend too much time on leisure things?

# Time for Work, Time for Play

In our daily lives there has to be a balance between work and leisure. When children used to have to work all day in the mines or in the mills, it was discovered that 'all work and no play makes Jack a dull boy'. We need to have time off so that we can do our work better, but we also need to work hard to justify having time off. How does God mean us to apportion our time?

---

### GOD'S WEEK

According to the old story, God worked for six days and rested on the seventh (= the sabbath). 'You have six days in which to do your work, but the seventh day is a day of rest dedicated to me', said the Lord. 'On that day no-one is to work' (Exodus 20:9–10). Such a pattern may not be possible today, but it is necessary for everybody to have at least one full day off each week— a day of rest.

When Jesus rose from the dead that first Easter Day, the first day of the week (Sunday) replaced the seventh day (Saturday). Sunday should be first of all a day for celebrating Jesus' resurrection. It is a good day to go to church and be re-created (= recreated). If we can make Sunday a day for physical, mental and spiritual change, we will go back to our everyday life with renewed energy and enthusiasm.

---

For many people today, the working week is less than six days and for some (the unemployed) there is no working week at all. This means that there has to be much more leisure activity for people. Make sure that your time off is spent in a useful—and not wasteful— way. Go walking or swimming or play a game, take up a hobby or do some study, find some meaningful occupation in addition to reading, listening to music or watching television. If you are unemployed, keep trying to find work and make sure that you have something special you do each day. If you cannot get paid employment, see if there are any opportunities for voluntary work where you live.

67

# Work—the Christian attitude towards it

Work is in God's plan for us—according to the Bible. The first man and woman were not intended to idle their time away. 'The Lord God placed the man in the Garden of Eden to cultivate it and guard it!' (Genesis 2:15). It was only after they had been put out of the garden for eating the forbidden fruit that God told them, 'You will have to work hard and sweat to make the soil produce anything' (Genesis 3:19). Work then became a toil and not an enjoyment.

When Jesus came into the world, he transformed the whole idea of work. Although he was the Son of God, he became a carpenter, at first apprenticed to his father Joseph and then working on his own. In so doing, he demonstrated that work need not be a sweat or a toil—it can be something enjoyable and purposeful.

## A CHRISTIAN ATTITUDE TO WORK

(1) It is something we do for God—and in partnership with God. 'Whatever you do,' said Paul, 'work at it with all your heart, as though you were working for the Lord and not for men' (Colossians 3:23). But Paul also says, 'We are partners working together for God' (1 Corinthians 3:9).

It is told of Sir Christopher Wren, the architect of St Paul's Cathedral in London, that as it was being built, he would walk among the men working on it and ask them what they were doing. As none of them knew him personally, he got honest answers! 'Carrying heavy stones,' said one of the men. 'Earning a miserable 3/6d [approximately 18p] a day,' said another. But a third worker said, 'I am helping a man called Christopher Wren to build a cathedral'.

(2) It is an opportunity to use the talents and abilities that God has given us. Moses called on all the craftsmen among the Israelites to use their artistic skills to make the tabernacle (= tent), where God lived during their years in the wilderness, a place that would be worthy of him. (See Exodus 35:30–36:1) We may not have specialised skills but God has given us all abilities that we can use in our work in the world.

68

# Work—how to serve Christ in it

Most Christians see their vocation in terms of their secular (= non-religious) employment. This is the work they believe that God means them to do. As Paul said to the Christian converts in Corinth, 'Each one of you should go on living according to the Lord's gift to him, and as he was when God called him' (1 Corinthians 7:17). Some Christians feel, however, that God is calling them to serve the Church in a full-time capacity. They are in a sense following the example of Andrew and Peter, the fishermen to whom Jesus said, 'Come with me, and I will teach you to catch men' (Matthew 4:19). Here are some ways in which you might be able to give such service.

The Christian ministry offers openings and opportunities for both men and women. It is one of the caring professions and is often regarded as a calling or a vocation rather than just a job. Most Churches require candidates for the ministry to have an academic training which may last up to five or six years, and there is usually a selection process to assess the suitability of candidates. Most ministers work in a parish situation, either on their own or as part of a team. Here they look after the spiritual needs of people. Others do specialised work as chaplains in industry, in hospitals, in universities and colleges, in prisons or in the armed forces. Some become teachers of religious education while others are full-time evangelists.

There are other forms of service with the Church as deacons, deaconesses and lay missionaries. Some serve the Church overseas as ministers, doctors, nurses, teachers, accountants, builders, and so on. Information about jobs with the Church can be obtained from the Publicity Department at the particular Church's headquarters. [The Church of Scotland Offices are at 121 George Street, Edinburgh, EH2 4YN.]

# It just needs money

'If I were a rich man . . . '

So sings Tevye in the musical, 'Fiddler on the Roof'. Many people have dreams of becoming rich and being able to buy things that they can't afford at the time. The purchase of goods is now made much simpler with the availability of credit cards, easy payment schemes, and suchlike. This, however, has its dangers. If you can't pay back when payments become due, interest is added to your balance and you find yourself having to pay much more than the original cost of the item.

Here are two thoughts about money from a Christian point-of-view.

## All Money comes originally from God
Money is simply the value of what you can purchase with it, like a meal in a restaurant, a journey on a bus, a pair of shoes or a loaf of bread. Take the loaf of bread that you buy in a supermarket or from a baker's shop. Where did it come from originally? It came from God, as this verse illustrates:

> Back of the loaf is the snowy flour,
> Back of the flour, the mill,
> Back of the mill is the wheat and the shower
> And the sun and the Father's will.

## All Money is a Gift from God
'God gives a man wealth' (Ecclesiastes 5:19). He gives him the skills and abilities with which to earn money. Even money that has not been personally earned, for example inherited wealth, has come from someone's earnings in the past. In a very real sense, then, all money is a gift from God.

70

# ... but it has its dangers

Money is said to be a good servant but a bad master. We can become so obsessed by money that nothing becomes more important to us than to acquire it. Paul warns people that 'the love of money is the root of all evil' (1 Timothy 6:10, AV).

---

### WHY DO WE GAMBLE?

People gamble because they believe that the money they may win will give them happiness. For some, gambling is big business. For most people it is a bit of fun. It is, however, potentially dangerous. It can become obsessive.

The compulsive gambler is his or her own worst enemy. Bigger and bigger stakes are played for and, instead of leading to a better way of life, gambling can sometimes lead to a life of misery and hardship.

Some Churches disapprove of gambling in any form— even raffles where the money is given to help a charity. Other Churches, like the Roman Catholic Church, see no harm in this form of gambling as long as essential payments to the Church have been met.

Gambling is by definition 'playing games of chance for money'. Do you think it is ever right? Or do you think it is completely un-Christian?

---

The Gospels are full of illustrations of the wrong use of money:

(a) Jesus met a wealthy young man who discovered that money doesn't make you happy. When he asked what to do, Jesus told him to sell all his possessions and give the money to the poor. The man couldn't do it and he remained unhappy. See Luke 18:18–25.

(b) Jesus told a story about a businessman who spent his whole life making money and then discovered that he couldn't take it with him when he died. How do you think he felt? See Luke 12:13–21.

(c) Jesus told another story about a man whose wealth blinded him to the needs of a beggar. After his death he suffered for his neglect in the fires of hell. See Luke 16:19–31.

71

# How we should use our money

If all our money comes originally from God, then surely we should use it in ways that would meet with God's approval. Here are some guidelines to help you.

## USE IT IN THE WORK OF THE WORLD

The world is God's world. Jesus said about it, 'Be concerned above everything else with the Kingdom of God and what he requires of you . . .' (Matthew 6:33). To live in God's world at all, the basic expenses of living have to be paid for—like a house to live in, food, clothes, electricity, gas, and so on—but the Kingdom of God is also about our 'brother in need' (1 John 3:17) and how we can support him. As a Christian, what would you see as the first claims on your money?

## USE IT IN THE WORK OF THE CHURCH

The work of the Church depends entirely on the support of its members. Major costs in a local congregation are the church buildings and their maintenance, heating and lighting. There are also expenses in running organisations, in paying for equipment, in purchasing books, Bibles and hymn books, and suchlike.

Another large part in the expenditure of a Church is the salary (= in Scotland, 'stipend') of a minister and the cost of a manse (= a minister's house). The minister is usually the only full-time employee of a congregation but there may be other paid appointments, for example an assistant minister, an organist, a church officer.

Another cost to take into account is the wider work of the Church which includes the payment of salaries to chaplains in factories, shipyards, colleges and universities, of teachers to train the leaders of the Church, and of nurses and social workers to run homes for the elderly, the young and those with special problems. Money is also needed to pay for missionaries and their partners to work with the Church overseas.

72

# ...and a guide to Church giving

Perhaps you are wondering how much you ought to contribute towards the work of the Church and what are the best methods of doing it.

## HOW MUCH TO GIVE...

In thinking what you should give to the Church, it is worth considering what you pay out in annual subscriptions or in purchasing periodicals or newspapers. Does it bear any comparison to your church givings? It is a good thing to think of your contribution to the Church's work as a percentage of the money that you earn or receive. In Old Testament times, the practice was to give a tithe (= a tenth) of your income. There is no rule about this today but it would be interesting for you to calculate what percentage of your income you are giving to the Church.

Jesus was sitting one day near the place in the temple where people put in their offerings. He watched many of the wealthy people put in a lot of money and then he saw a poor widow come along and drop in two small copper coins. He called his disciples and said to them, 'I tell you that this poor widow  put more in the offering box than all the others. The others put in what they had to spare of their riches; but she, poor as she is, put in all she had—she gave all she had to live on' (Mark 12:43–44).

A good guide to giving is to ask yourself—Is what I am giving hurting me? Is it a sacrifice? If not, perhaps you are not giving enough.

## AND HOW TO GIVE

The Church's work must be supported week after week. The Weekly Freewill Offering envelope system encourages regular giving. You get a packet of 52 dated envelopes to cover each Sunday in the year. You may prefer to give your offering monthly through a Bankers' Order or by paying an annual cheque. If you pay tax, there is considerable benefit to the Church if you give your offering by Deed of Covenant. The Church Treasurer will give you details.

# Other ways of supporting the Church

A lot of help can be given to the Church on a voluntary basis. Here are some possible ways in which you may be able to give some Christian service in your local church or community.

Every church needs people who are willing to teach in a Sunday School or Bible Class, or perhaps to help with a youth club or uniformed organisation. Many churches too need help with playgroups and mother and toddler groups. Or there may be a house group, a Bible study group or a prayer group that you could join.

Can you sing or play a musical instrument? If you have got talent of this kind, there is sure to be some way in which it can be used in your church—leading the praise at a Sunday service or in giving entertainment. Others have skills in some trade or craft or can work as gardeners or labourers. In every church there is work to be done around the buildings or in the grounds.

Or perhaps there is need in your congregation for a secretary or for clerical work. Can you type or use a duplicating machine or a photocopier? If you are good at writing, what about helping with the church magazine?

The Church is all about people, lonely people, people in need, people wanting to be visited. What about taking flowers or magazines to the housebound or helping with a lunch club? There may be opportunities for you to do this within your church and/or in the local community.

74

# The Gospel and the World

## The Gospel—Sharing it with the World

If this book has helped you to find a faith in Jesus Christ, you will want to share this faith with others. The Gospel is not something that we should keep to ourselves.

---

### SHARING THE GOOD NEWS

The city of Samaria was being besieged by the Syrian army which had put up its tents outside the walls. Four lepers who were not allowed into the city wandered into the camp one night and found it deserted. The enemy had fled, leaving behind them food, clothing and also silver and gold. The lepers couldn't believe their good luck. They ate and drank what they could and then hid some of their trophies. Then one of them remembered their fellow-Israelites in the city. 'We shouldn't be doing this,' he said, 'we have good news and we shouldn't keep it to ourselves.' So although they were lepers, they went into the city and told people what they had found. (The whole story can be found in 2 Kings 7:3–10.)

---

Have you ever tried gossiping the Gospel? What about being a 'Good News' vendor? If you have an opportunity to speak about your faith, be ready 'to explain the hope you have in you' (1 Peter 3:15). Even if you are not too sure about your beliefs, 'do not be worried about what you will say for the Holy Spirit will teach you at that time what you should say' (Luke 12:11).

## The Gospel—Living it out in the World

We do not share our faith only in what we say but in the concern we have for the world and its needs. This book does not attempt to deal with many matters that must concern us as Christians, for example the whole problem of poverty and deprivation. 'You will always have poor people with you,' said Jesus (Matthew 26:11). Equally it does not deal with matters like war and peace, violence and vandalism, cancer and medical research, pollution and the environment. In the next few pages there is space to look at only *some* of the more personal issues that can affect Christians in their everyday lives.

75

# Addiction

Things to which one can become addicted include drugs, smoking and alcohol. In the first instance such things are attractive because they supply a need or help with a problem, for example loneliness. Addiction, however, creates more problems than it solves. Sometimes it leads to death. As Christians, we should act responsibly—not only as individuals—but in how we present this to other people. 'Decide never to do anything that would make your brother stumble or fall into sin' (Romans 14:13).

## DRUGS
Drugs are very valuable, medically speaking, in that they can give relief from pain and help restore health. They should never be taken unless prescribed by a doctor. Here are some drugs that can have very dangerous consequences if taken irresponsibly.

STIMULANTS: like Amphetamines, which make you feel good but produce high blood pressure and lead to tension.
SEDATIVES: like Barbiturates, which relax the nerves and get rid of anxiety but can have painful withdrawal symptoms.
HALLUCINOGENS: like LSD or Cannabis, which can send you on a pleasant 'trip' but will have disturbing after-effects.
NARCOTICS: like Morphine and Heroin, which can kill pain and give you a feeling of confidence, but can also make you very ill.

Solvent Abuse or Glue Sniffing is a drug problem for many young teenagers. The effect is similar to getting drunk but the side-effects can include rashes and sores, nightmares, depression and loss of appetite.

A drug-addict cannot easily get off drugs. He or she tends to live only for the next 'fix' and, if necessary, will steal money to buy it. Anyone who misuses drugs requires medical help, but the police should also be informed so that the pusher who is supplying the drugs can be caught.

## SMOKING
People smoke because it relieves tension and can be socially desirable. It is also seen by some young people as a sign that they are growing up. The nicotine in tobacco can be chewed as well as smoked. It is addictive and can cause cancer of the mouth, throat, lungs and bladder as well as heart disease.

76

# Addiction

## ALCOHOL

As a chemical, alcohol can be useful. It can be used for cleaning purposes. However, when consumed, it is potentially very harmful. There is more alcohol in spirits and liqueurs than in beer or lager, but even small amounts of alcohol can affect you when it gets into the bloodstream. Alcohol makes people feel less inhibited and more sociable. This is the attraction. If we drink, however, we can find that we are no longer in control of our speech, our vision or our movements. That is why it is not only dangerous—but illegal—to drink and then drive.

Alcohol is addictive. An alcoholic will get to the stage where he or she cannot survive without a drink. Even people who only drink a little may find that they can't do anything with confidence without first having a drink. Alcohol can be very damaging to the health and causes great problems for anyone suffering from the disease. For alcoholics who really want to kick the habit, there is an organisation known as Alcoholics Anonymous. Support for their families is available through Al-Anon and Alateen, the latter for young people.

The Bible doesn't completely condemn the drinking of alcohol. It points out that God gives 'wine to gladden the hearts of the people' (Psalm 104:15, REB). Paul also says that it is advisable to 'take a little wine to help your digestion' (1 Timothy 5:23). Wine is the fruit of the vine and in Jesus' day was a normal form of drink. At the last supper, it was used as a symbol of Christ's blood.

The Bible also, however, makes mention of the dangers of alcohol. 'Don't let wine tempt you, even though it is rich red, though it sparkles in the cup, and it goes down smoothly. The next morning you will feel as if you had been bitten by a poisonous snake' (Proverbs 23:31–32). And Paul has to tell the Christians in Ephesus—'Do not get drunk with wine, which will only ruin you; instead be filled with the Spirit' (Ephesians 5:18). We have to make up our own minds whether to be teetotal (= abstain completely from alcohol) or drink only in moderation.

# Love   Marriage   Sex

The above words have been put in alphabetical order—but is it the right order?

In India, where many marriages are arranged by parents, the order would be

### MARRIAGE SEX LOVE

The traditional order in the West is

### LOVE MARRIAGE SEX

The actual order today is very often

### SEX LOVE MARRIAGE

As Christians, we must put Love first. Even in the New Testament, however, love has many different meanings. It can mean Friendship, Affection, Sexual Attraction and Sharing Love. Falling in love is an emotional experience in which two people of the opposite sex are attracted to each other. This can develop into a friendship which can become closer and more intimate as the affection they have for each other grows. If they have been 'going steady' for a long time, they may reach the point where they want to share their love for each other completely and commit themselves to one another in marriage.

Physical sex is a natural part of this relationship. God made us male and female. For some people, however, this can present problems. A Christian is not free to have an intimate sexual relationship except with his or her married partner. A homo-sexual relationship, that is, a sexual relationship between people of the same sex, is also wrong. In Hebrews 13:4 we are reminded that 'God will judge those who are immoral'. Such relationships also create a health hazard and this is particularly evident in the growth of AIDS. Where such relationships do exist, however, a great deal of Christian understanding must be exercised. The ideal for all couples is a happy and healthy sexual partnership within the framework of marriage.

# 'For better, for worse'

## CHRISTIAN MARRIAGE

Legally, you can be married in a Registrar's office or in a church. Marriage is simply an agreement or covenant in which a man and a woman pledge themselves to each other for the rest of their lives. Being married in church does not in itself guarantee that the marriage will be successful. It is, however, an acknowledgement by the couple that God is there and will bless them in the union they are about to make.

## THE PURPOSES OF MARRIAGE

(1)  Marriage is for the happiness, help and comfort which a husband and wife will be able to give to each other. It is part of God's plan for mankind. 'It is not good,' he said, 'for man to live alone. I will make a suitable companion to help him' (Genesis 2:18).

(2)  Marriage is to provide a proper setting for a man and a woman to have an intimate relationship with each other. 'That is why a man leaves his father and mother and is united with his wife, and they become one [= one flesh, AV]' (Genesis 2:24). It is wrong for a couple to 'live together' if they are not married.

(3)  Marriage is for the procreation or production of children and should provide the kind of environment in which they can have a secure and happy upbringing.

(4)  Marriage is a commitment in which a husband and wife promise that they will be faithful to each other for the rest of their lives. They take each other 'to have and to hold ... for better, for worse, for richer, for poorer, in sickness and in health ....' All too many marriages nowadays end in divorce and this is always regrettable. Paul made it clear in 1 Corinthians 7:11 that 'a husband must not divorce his wife'.

## MIXED MARRIAGES

A mixed marriage is usually one between a Roman Catholic and a Protestant, or it could be between a Christian and a Hindu, or a Moslem. Anyone contemplating such a marriage should recognise that there may be difficulties, especially in the area of religious belief and the bringing up of children.

# Last Things

As we come to the last pages of this book, let us look at some of the last things we are likely to talk about, including death and what happens after we die.

## DEATH—THE ONE CERTAIN FACT

There was once a king called Philip who ordered his slave to wake him every morning with the words, 'Philip, remember that you must die!' Death is not something that we would want to be reminded of each day but it is still the one 'fact of life' which we cannot disregard. At the end of our life here, all of us must die.

Because what happens after we die is an unknown factor, we have a natural fear of death. In Job 18:14 (AV), death is described as 'the king of terrors'. 'To die,' said Peter Pan, 'will be an awfully big adventure'. But, we may ask, how awful will it be?

## IS THERE LIFE AFTER DEATH?

We must first ask the question whether there is life after death. 'If a man dies, shall he live again?' (Job 14:14, RSV). Something within us tells us that there is an immortal (= a non-dying) side to all of us. When we die, our physical body is returned to its elements, 'dust to dust, ashes to ashes'—either following cremation or a burial—but is there not something that remains and survives?

We cannot conceive of life after death in terms of our experience here. Nor would we want it to be just a continuation of the present kind of existence. What Christians describe as heaven is not a life controlled by the clock or the calendar but a different kind of life altogether.

When we are in the company of someone we love and of someone who loves us, then life takes on a new dimension. Time doesn't matter. We are in the realm of the eternal. Our experience then becomes a little like that of John Newton in the hymn 'Amazing Grace'.

> When we've been here ten thousand years,
>   Bright shining as the sun,
> We've no less days to sing God's praise
>   Than when we first began!

# Last Things

## A CHRISTIAN UNDERSTANDING OF THE AFTER-LIFE

For a Christian, belief about the after-life is tied up with belief in Jesus. Even on this earth his life had an 'eternal' quality about it. 'I am the resurrection and the life,' he said, 'whoever believes in me will live, even though he dies; and whoever lives and believes in me will never die' (John 11:25–26).

After his crucifixion, Jesus rose again. What his disciples experienced then gave reality to what Jesus had said about himself as 'the resurrection and the life'. 'For forty days after his death he appeared to them many times in ways that proved beyond doubt that he was alive' (Acts 1:3). His resurrection appearances, however, were unique. Clearly he was no longer bound by time or space. At the same time, he was recognisable as the man whom they had known before his death.

Jesus' resurrection, Paul says, is 'the guarantee that those who sleep in death will also be raised' (1 Corinthians 15:20). This means that those who die believing in Christ share in some way in his resurrection. Their resurrection, however, will be different. Thus to the question 'What kind of body will they have?' (1 Corinthians 15:35), Paul replies by drawing a comparison between a seed buried in the ground and the beautiful flower that it becomes. As a flower, it has a different 'body' from when it was a seed. So, says Paul, 'when the body is buried, it is a physical body; when raised, it will be a spiritual body' (1 Corinthians 15:42,44).

## ...AND WHAT IT WILL BE LIKE

We are not meant to investigate the after-life. To his anxious disciples, Jesus said, 'Do not be worried and upset. Believe in God and believe also in me. There are many rooms in my Father's house, and I am going to prepare a place for you' (John 14:1–2). For those who put their trust in God, the Negro spiritual reminds us that in heaven there will be 'plenty good room'.

We must try to think of heaven—not so much as a place—as being 'at home with the Lord' (2 Corinthians 5:8). We are in the area of relationships rather than of regions. If we know that God loves and cares for us, then we know we will be safe with him whatever happens.

81

# Church Membership

This book has tried to outline what it means to be a Christian and a communicant member of the Christian Church. The membership vows may vary from Church to Church but they will be basically the same. Below are listed the vows asked by two of the larger Churches in Britain.

## CHURCH OF SCOTLAND

(1) Do you believe in one God, Father, Son and Holy Spirit, and do you confess Jesus Christ as your Saviour and Lord?

(2) Do you promise to join regularly with your fellow Christians in worship on the Lord's Day?

(3) Do you promise to be faithful in reading the Bible and in prayer?

(4) Do you promise to give a fitting proportion of your time, talents and money for the Church's work in the world?

(5) Do you promise, depending on the grace of God, to confess Christ before men and women, to serve him in your daily work and to walk in his ways all the days of your life?

## UNITED REFORMED CHURCH

(1) Do you confess your faith in one God, Father, Son and Holy Spirit, taking the Father to be your Father,
the Son to be your Saviour and Lord,
and the Spirit to be your Helper and Guide?

(2) Do you promise, in dependence on God's grace, to be faithful in private and public worship; to live in the fellowship of the Church and to share in its work; and to give and serve, as God enables you, for the advancement of his Kingdom throughout the world?

(3) Do you promise, by that same grace, to follow Christ and to seek to do and to bear his will all the days of your life?

(4) Do you trust in his mercy alone to bring you into the fulness of the world to come?